FLORISTRY COMPETITIONS
The ultimate guide for competitors, judges and stewards.

ABOUT THE AUTHOR

Lynda Owen NDSF, FSF has been a professional florist for over forty years. During this time she has been an ardent competitor in floristry competitions. Amongst the many trophies she has won are two Gold medals for the Interflora exhibit at the RHS Chelsea Flower Show and a Gold Medal at the RHS Hampton Court Flower Show, together with the trophy for the best exhibit in the Professional Floristry category at the RHS Chelsea Flower Show.

Since becoming a floristry judge Lynda has travelled extensively both in Great Britain and the world, judging competitions and teaching floristry. She judged the World Cup of Floristry in The Netherlands in 1997, Eurofleurs competition in Italy in 2002 and the National Floristry Championships in Russia in 2006. In Great Britain she has had the honour of judging at the RHS Chelsea Flower Show, UK Skills Floristry competitions, Interflora and British Florist Association national competitions, and many more.

Lynda is a member of the European Federation of Professional Judges and one of the founder members of the UK Floristry Judges Guild. She has also been the manager for the British competitor David Ragg in the Europa Cup in 2005, the British competitor David Denyer in the World Cup in 2004 and the British competitor Neil Whittaker in the World cup in 2010.

Lynda is the author of two books 'Wedding Floristry' and 'The Contemporary Flower Arranger' and writes extensively for many publications.

Lynda lives in Worcester, England with her husband Ray. She has one son Tim, two cats and a host of floristry friends.

Dedication

In memory of those past floristry judges who laid the foundations of judging excellence and to the competitors who made it all possible.

Acknowledgments

Special thanks go to Pam Simcock, NDSF, FSF and Isabel Wilton, NDSF, FSF for their dedication, loyalty, friendship, unstinting support and expert floristry judging knowledge whilst compiling this book.

A big thank you to Tracy Tomlinson, NDSF, FSF, Chairman of the UK Floristry Judges Guild, for the invaluable advice and help with revision.

Grateful thanks to my friend Bryan Wedge, F.C.A., for proofreading the book and putting in the commas in the correct places.

And finally my love and thanks to Ray and Tim for their never ending support for all my projects.

I would like to acknowledge the sterling work of Eric Roberts who wrote the Interflora guidance notes for student judges - *Eric Roberts 1978*

Table of contents

FOR COMPETITORS

Chapter 1: Why have floristry competitions?
Benefits of entering a floristry competition..................................12
Benefits of staff entering a competition...................................... 13

Chapter 2: How to enter a floristry competition
So you think you would like to enter a floristry competition?......14
Tips for entering floristry competitions...15
My competition resources 16

Chapter 3: How to become the winner
Choosing a competition to enter... 17
Levels of competition... 18
Tips to becoming the winner..19

Chapter 4: Mental Preparation
Yes, I can win..20
Competition timetable 22

Chapter 5: How to read the schedule and follow the rules
Use your imagination 23
Abide by the rules... 23
The wording holds clues... 26
Tips 26

Chapter 6: How to understand what the judge is looking for
What makes a florist a floral designer?....................................... 27
Understanding the design techniques.. 28
Idea 30
Colour and colour wheel.. 31
Composition 32
Technique 33
Conclusion.. 33

Table of contents

Chapter 7: Design tips and common faults
General design tips 35
Design shapes made simple 36
How to gain more marks for colour 37
Winning tips for bridal designs and body accessorie 37
Hand tied designs 38
Flower arrangement tip 40
Funeral tribute advice 41
Planted design guidelines 41
My own designs 42

Chapter 8: Surprise/Mystery competitions
Practice makes perfect 44
Open and closed judging 45
Tips on how to win 45

Chapter 9: Competing overseas
Aide Memoire 47
Open judging 48
After the competition 48

Chapter 10: After the competition
After competition tips 49
How to be a good winner 50
How to be a good loser 50

FOR JUDGES

Chapter 11: What is a floristry judge?
How to become a floristry judge 52
The qualities of a good floristry judge 53
Training to be a judge 53
Continuous professional development 53

Chapter 12: The judges code of conduct
Judges code of ethics 54
Judging criteria 56

Chapter 13: Judges training
Practical sessions 57
Continuous professional development 58
Shadow judging 58

Chapter 14: How to prepare for a judging assignment
Check all information 59
Reading the schedules 60
Essential judging kit 61
At the venue 61

Chapter 15: Awarding marks
A fine balancing act 62
Marks out of ten 63
Who will be the winner? 63
Marking sheets 64
Respect of plant material 65
Finding the winner 65

Chapter 16: In the competition room
A helping hand 66
Out of schedule 67
Concentration 67
Evaluation 68
Completing marking sheets 68
Respecting competitors exhibits 69
Checking the marks 69
Written comments 70

Chapter 17: The Commentary
First impressions 71
Conviction and confidence 71
Practicing 72
Speaking out 72
Stage fright 72
Structure of the commentary 73
The winners' form 74
Looking confident 75
Using a microphone 75
Quick tips for an effective commentary 76

Chapter 18: Talking to competitors
Points on how to give constructive criticism 77
Vocabulary 78
Using descriptive words 78
Words to inspire 79

Chapter 19: Team and open judging
Lead judge 83
How to be a dream team judge 84
Open judging 84

Chapter 20: The competition schedule
What is a floristry competition schedule?......85
Schedule preparation......85
Inspiring schedules......86
Discussion......87
Surprise/Mystery competitions......87
Key points when writing competition schedules......88

Chapter 21: Overseas judges
Lead judge......89
Material respect......90
Communication......90

FOR COMPETITION STEWARDS

Chapter 22: Stewarding a floristry competition
Stewarding at a heat......92
Stewarding a major competition or mystery item......93
Checklist for stewards......94

Bibliography:
For craftsmanship......95
For floristry inspiration......95
For environmental inspiration......95

Preface

*" Learn from yesterday, live for today, hope for tomorrow.
The important thing is not to stop questioning. "*
Albert Einstein

This book has taken me on a fascinating journey, a voyage of discovery into the world of floristry competitions and beyond, looking at competitions both from the viewpoint of competitors and judges. I hope this book will unravel some of the mysteries of floristry competitions for you the reader.

It has been exciting to delve into archives, talk to distinguished professional competitors and judges and search for clear and concise terminology to make this an interesting read for anyone entering or judging a floristry competition. It has brought me to the conclusion that both competitors and floristry judges share many of the same attributes. Floristry judges are not from another planet, and rather than hide judges from view there has to be an understanding and appreciation of what is involved in judging a competition, and the host of disciplines a floristry judge adheres to. Competitors and judges share a special bond, a passion for design, the love of flowers, and both are seeking excellence.

My wish is that you can dip in and out of this book easily and quickly to find the information you seek without reading the entire book. However if you choose to read the book from cover to cover I will be delighted. I hope you will be able to find everything you need to know about entering or judging a floristry competition here. I hope competitors will read the 'For Judges' section and have more understanding of the role of the judge, and judges will read the competitors section to refresh their memory and remember how it was to be a competitor.

Floristry competitions are where new techniques and designs evolve for the future; sometimes it's where long forgotten skills and designs are given a new lease of life. It's a hotbed of creativity, where art and craft combine to showcase the talent of professional florists to the world. It's the finest place to learn about floristry in fun, unity and friendship with other florists. Friends you make in floristry last a lifetime.

Floristry competitions cannot be seen in isolation, they have to change to meet the demands of the audience, as they are part of the broader picture of the floral industry as a whole. For too long the spectators at competitions have been irrelevant and there must be a real desire to bring floristry competitions to the forefront, this is the next big challenge. Targeting greater awareness of the skills of florists to the general public through floristry competitions will secure the future for generations of young florists.

From the start of floristry competitions there have been stalwart, dedicated expert florists prepared to give their time and knowledge freely and willingly in the pursuit of floristry excellence and to help their fellow florists.

Florists of long standing, who were deemed to be experts in their field, judged the first floristry competitions, but it soon became apparent that to achieve credibility amongst competitors some type of examination for floristry judges should take place. In 1970 a group of eminent florists within Interflora formed a committee to set up the first Diploma of Judging, and this created the basis for the national judging examination we use today.

Although I have collated the information in this book, the credit for much of it goes to the great judges and florists from the past that diligently recorded the development of floristry competitions and judging in all its aspects and passed on their valuable knowledge. Many of the words written nearly forty years ago are still as relevant today as they were then.

The pioneer florists who paved the way and formed the first judging qualification were;

- Mr Maurice Evans,
- Mrs Dorothy Gullick
- Mr Geoffrey Warren
- Miss Monica Sturge
- Mrs Rona Coleman
- Mr Jimmy Nuttall
- Mrs Elizabeth Murdoch
- Mr Joe Reilly
- And Major Eric Roberts who also prepared the 'Interflora Guidance Notes for Student Judges' in 1978 and many papers on floristry judging.

Following on from this inaugural examination Maurice Evans and Jean Siviter continued to thrust floristry judging to a new level of professionalism. We owe a debt of gratitude to these legendary florists and all those visionary floristry judges from Interflora, the Society of Floristry, the UK Floristry Judges Guild and other organisations that have passed on their expert knowledge eagerly and unstintingly.

Floristry competitions are a creative force, the pulse that drives the floristry industry forward, competitions empower florists and they are the lifeblood of a dynamic floral business.

Long may they continue, and good luck to all floristry competitors and judges.

FOR COMPETITORS

Chapter 1:
Why have floristry competitions?

" Only those who risk going too far can possibly find out how far they can go. "
TS Elliot

In this chapter:
- Benefits of entering a floristry competition
- Benefits of staff entering a competition

There is continuous competition in everyday life as a florist. On a personal level whether it's competing with fellow staff at the workbench to create the best floral design, achieving top marks in a college course, or making the biggest in-house sale; life for a florist is always competitive.

On a business level a florists shop is in competition with rival florists, supermarkets, market stalls and other retailers on a daily basis. Owners are always trying to secure additional sales, and being one step ahead of competitors is an essential ingredient for profitability.

Floristry competitions are vital for both personal growth and business development. Floristry is a very competitive, creative industry that is constantly shifting, it's a fashion craft governed by the economic climate, and prevailing styles in clothes and home decor. Styles in floristry cannot stand still, customers expect a high level of skill and design ability, and they thirst for new and exciting products. Therefore competitions are vital to thrust forward futuristic floral designs, and to maintain quality and expertise. In short, floristry competitions keep the industry ahead of its rivals. Today's avant garde competition design will be diluted into mainstream usability tomorrow, and every High Street store and florist will be clamouring for it.

New design has to start somewhere, and in floristry it's the competitions that initiate it.

The benefits of entering a floristry competition.

On a personal level this is your time to shine. Yes, you may be disappointed. Yes, it might be stressful. Yes, it will take time and energy to enter a competition, but the rewards you reap will far outweigh any minor considerations. You are reaching for a star and the exhilaration that comes when victory is within your grasp is immeasurable.

Henry Ford wrote, 'One of the greatest discoveries a man makes, one of his greatest surprises, is to find he can do what he was afraid he couldn't.'

For the competitor

- Enhance your personal floristry skills.
- Keep up to date with new techniques.
- Build your capacity to think creatively.
- Maintain your motivation.
- Remain familiar with the latest floristry design styles.
- Learn the discipline of creating a special order to a specific instruction.
- Gain expert tips from talking to the floristry judges.
- Analyse the winning entry in comparison to your design, and learn from any mistakes.
- Personal satisfaction.
- Win rewards, accolades and prizes.

The benefits of staff entering a floristry competition.

People generally enter floristry as a career because it's a creative industry. They love the flowers they work with, and the buzz they get from a clients emotional reaction to their designs.

The environment the employer creates will have a positive effect on the motivation of staff. Happy fulfilled workers mean a successful, thriving business. A workplace that is inspirational and allows staff to grow and reach their full potential will result in enhanced productivity.

Training and recognition is the key to a flourishing hothouse of expertise and enthusiasm, this will generate a sparkling fun shop to excite customers and produce more sales.

Encouraging and supporting employees to enter floristry competitions has a two-fold effect. It can help employees fulfil their dreams whilst building confidence and enthusiasm, and this will pay dividends for your business.

A floristry competition is a discipline like creating a specific design for a special shop order it needs concentration and expertise. Learning these values alone, plus staying in touch with new styles of design is a bonus that employers can ill afford to miss.

For the employer

- Networking - showing florists locally and beyond your shops specialist skills.
- Advertising for your business - both local and national.
- Creating a reputation for cutting edge floristry.
- Encouraging creativity in your shop.
- Motivating your staff - keeping them keen and interested.
- Learning new techniques and styles to pass on to customers.
- Valuable publicity
- Be ahead of rival businesses in skill and style.
- Generate an inspirational ethos in your shop, the buzz that comes from keen passionate florists.

Chapter 2:
How to enter a floristry competition

> *Fortune sides with him who dares.*
> Vergil

In this chapter:
- So you think you would like to enter a floristry competition?
- Tips for entering floristry competitions
- My competition resources

Entering floristry competitions is not always about winning the first prize, although obviously, this is the ultimate aim. It can be about doing your personal best, and achieving and learning from the competition experience. Mixing and chatting with other florists, picking up tips, exploring your competitive urge and enhancing your personal skills, this is rewarding in itself. For some competitors it's about stretching the boundaries of design and developing new techniques that gives them the buzz, winning is the icing on the cake.

Before competing

Before entering your first floristry competition go to visit competitions near you. Look carefully at the designs and talk to the competitors, this will help you understand the skills you need to compete. At the end of the competition listen to what the judge has to say about the entries in the room, don't be afraid to ask questions you will gain valuable information for when you start to compete. Build your knowledge about different varieties of plant material and write down the names of any unusual flowers.

Make notes at the end of this chapter to remind you of key points and vital knowledge you may need.

So you think you would like to enter a floristry competition?

Start by looking for competitions that are being held in your area, generally these are well advertised in floristry magazines. When entering your first competition choose one that is appropriate for your level of skill and expertise. Don't be over ambitious, start in a small way and build up to highflying competitions.

Tips for entering floristry competitions

- Read the rules; make sure you are eligible to enter. There may be an age limit or experience maximum.
- If there is a cut off date for entries make sure you apply in plenty of time. Late entries may not be accepted.
- Read the schedule carefully and understand what is required. More people fail because they do not read the schedule carefully than for any other reason.
- If you are unsure about the wording of the schedule send a question to the organiser.
- Start planning your design early, sketch it first and then practice, practice, practice.
- Use only the best quality materials; dead flowers do not win competitions.
- Condition all the flowers and foliage properly and leave to have a good drink before using.
- Keep focused and make sure that you allow plenty of time to make your competition entry. You will be surprised how long this will take.
- Pack your floristry entry really well for travelling. If it is damaged on route all your hard work is in vain.
- Arrive at the competition venue in plenty of time to stage your exhibit.
- Make sure you tell the competition steward you have arrived and you are allocated a competition number.
- Stage your entry simply and neatly, spray with water if necessary.
- Don't leave your entry for someone else to bring home, stay and listen to what the judges have to say.

Good luck, enjoy, and have fun competing.

Chapter 2: How to enter a floristry competition

My competition resources

Use this page to record any information you learn from viewing floristry competitions.

❀ Great advice:

Mistakes to avoid:

Important points to remember:

Clever tips:

Flower, foliage and plant variety names:

Recommended books to read:

❀ Great advice:

Mistakes to avoid:

Important points to remember:

Clever tips:

Flower, foliage and plant variety names:

Recommended books to read:

Chapter 3:
How to become the winner

"They conquer who believe they can."
Ralph Waldo Emerson

In this chapter:
- Choosing a competition to enter
- Levels of competition
- Tips to becoming the winner

To win a floristry competition there has to be a combination of skills, but most of all there has to be commitment. From the moment the competition schedule arrives it will be your motivation and single-minded focus that will be the key to winning. To win a floristry competition not only means you need an abundance of floristry skills you also need mental fitness. The winning competitor will have the determination and perseverance to keep going and build momentum.

Floristry competitions are all purely performance competitions, where winning or losing is based solely on the competitor's ability to produce the best design in the competition room on the day. Generally the competitor will not know what their opponent's capabilities are. At other times they may know by reputation who the other contestants are, but the judges will determine on the day, purely on the competition exhibits in front of them, who will be the winner. The reputation of your competitors should not affect your confidence or motivation; if you are at peak performance and focused you have as much opportunity to win as your rivals.

Choosing a competition to enter

- The first type of floristry competition is where you make the design in the comfort of your own workroom and then take the competition piece to the venue already made. This is perhaps the easiest competition to enter because you will have the time and relaxed atmosphere of familiar surroundings to make the exhibit.
- The second type of competition is where you know the schedule in advance and you take all the flowers, foliage and sundries to make the item, but the actual design is made at the competition venue, generally within a given timescale. Here the advantage is that you can practice the exhibit in the workroom many times and within the timescale allowed. Sometimes there is more than one design to make in this type of competition and the designs will be displayed in a booth. A final display mark is often given for the overall placement and effect of all the pieces arranged together.

- The surprise or mystery competition, sometimes called 'A Pandora's Box,' is where you make a design from an unseen schedule, and from unseen flowers, foliage and sundries. The design is usually made in a specific timescale, and often you have around fifteen minutes to view the flowers and foliage before starting the design. There are usually strictly observed rules applied to this type of competition with regard to the use of tools and equipment. Often in this style of competition the designs are made in front of an audience. This is the most difficult type of competition of all - it takes a cool head. You need to take control and have a great level of floristry skill and creativity.

Levels of competitions

There are levels of competition to suit all competitors. From beginners with less than three years experience where competence in technique and workmanship feature highly to talented, experienced designer competitions, where conceptual organic installations catapult floristry into art.

Free expression competitions where the competitors are given a theme to work to are where designer florists can let their imagination blossom, within an interpretative theme. This type of competition is more than being a competent florist; it's about thinking and creating like an artist, taking floristry to another level.

A team of designers/artists working in the natural environment to create unique organic creations generally undertake Land Art or Earth Art competitions. Making structures, earthworks and installations with organic material directly into the landscape is leading edge art. This is conceptual design of the highest level.

Tips of how to become a winner

- Read and dissect the competition schedule.
- Follow the rules of the competition otherwise face disqualification or penalties.
- Analyse the judging facets and where maximum marks can be gained. This is the criterion that the competition judges will adhere to.
- Learn, understand and use the principles and elements of good design.
- Have a mental plan, visualise your finished design, sketch ideas.
- Practice, practice, practice, a winning design is not whipped up in a few minutes.
- Be adventurous, expand your ideas, and push the boundaries within the framework and principles of good design.
- Stay focused, be positive, and keep motivation levels high.
- Don't change designs in midstream, particularly if it is a surprise competition. Try to keep going with the original design and work it out.
- Be technically competent, your design will only win if it is perfectly executed, finished and polished to the highest degree.
- Use only perfect flowers and foliage, and condition all materials well to ensure long lasting qualities.
- Don't over accessorise. The flowers and plant material should tell the story.
- Don't overload the design with too many gimmicky design ideas; one clever design concept is enough.
- Pace yourself; know how much time you have to make the competition work and allocate time wisely to ensure the design can be finished perfectly on time.
- Have a clear, simple, mental map,

Evaluate, Plan, Organise, Execute, WIN.

Chapter 4:
Mental preparation
YES I CAN WIN

" Skill and confidence are an unconquered army. "
George Hubert

In this chapter:
🌸 Competition timetable

Examine the reasons why you have entered a floristry competition. The motivation may be to be the best, the incentive might be prize money or to defeat all opponents, one thing is for sure, you want to win the competition.

There will be external distractions that need to be eliminated, making a competition piece whilst others are out partying, or missing a family event because it falls on a competition day will be likely, remember success often comes at a price.

Sacrifices in your personal life may have to be made and there could be monetary costs involved in entering a competition. Travelling to and from a competition, the flowers and foliage you use together with the sundries all add up, so be prepared to spend money.

Competition fitness means floristry skills and mental strength. Plan as though going into battle and have single-minded focus. Read the floristry competition schedule and then;

EVALUATE
PLAN
ORGANISE
EXECUTE
WIN

You will need motivation, focus, determination, perseverance, visualisation, endurance, technical skill and design creativity to win a floristry competition.

Thinking and planning are essential if you want to win.

- You must really want to win more than anything else.
- Plan practice sessions and don't miss them.
- Before the competition keep distractions to a minimum, purely focus on the competition ahead.
- When the going gets tough, be mentally tough.
- If it's harder than you thought then this is a great opportunity to show what you can do. Don't let it slip away.
- Don't become over confident and think its easy, give your all.
- You will only push yourself to the limit if your mind allows you to, there has to be a strong and resounding purpose to win.
- Sports men and women chant a mantra in their minds before a competition - it's a touchstone to remind them of their purpose and it puts the mind at ease.
  (A mantra is a little saying that calms and helps you stay focused.)
- Imagine that success is realistic and you will be a success.
- Stay focused even when the competition takes you out of your comfort zone.
- Mentally rehearse the forthcoming experience, this has a tangible effect on performance and will help you stay focused.
- Remember this is a life enhancing experience - enjoy it.
- Don't flag toward the end; keep up the motivation and focus. This is where mental endurance pays dividends.
- Do everything to make sure you mentally peak just before the competition. Now is the time to focus only on the positive aspects of your potential.
- Don't have the lead and then blow it at the end, keep going full on, victory is nearly yours.

NEVER GIVE UP

Make a timetable similar to the one used here to help you organise your practice time, Planning should start the minute you receive the competition schedule, and organising a timetable means you will not run out of practice time.

COMPETITION TIMETABLE

Date:	Action:
	Send in the entry form.
	Schedule arrives, Evaluate, read and dissect. Write down the major features in the schedule.
	Ask any questions regarding the schedule early, there may be a cut off point for questions and answers.
	Plan by sketching and start to practice. Take photos of finished design and analyse them. Pin these photos up above your work space for reference.
	Organise your time efficiently, have at least two mock ups of the competition piece.
	A days rest before the competition.
	Execute the competition entry.
	WIN THE COMPETITION

Chapter 5:
How to read the schedule and follow the rules of the competition

"Beware that you do not lose the substance by grasping at the shadow."
Aesop

In this chapter:
- Use your imagination
- Abide by the rules
- The wording holds clues
- Tips

More people fail in competitions because they have not read the schedule correctly than for any other reason. The floristry competition schedule is a discipline to work to, if you choose to ignore the wording then the possibility is that you will be disqualified or be given penalty points.

The competition schedule is there to help both competitors and judges. It does not include any hidden meanings; it is a straightforward instruction that has been written carefully to avoid any disputes. Sometimes competitors try to read into the schedule something that is not there.

Use your imagination

Read the competition schedule thoroughly and analyse every word, then use your imagination and creativity to design an innovative entry within the confines of the schedule.

Abide by the rules

It is a total waste of your time and money if you ignore the rules and face being 'out of schedule.' Check any size limitations carefully, if you are unsure about any wording there is generally a technical committee or appointed judge who can provide an answer to your question.

Technical committee

For national and world competitions there is generally an appointed technical committee or jury. The role of a technical committee can vary depending on the competition organisers and the country the competition is being held in. A technical committee is made up of three or more experienced professional floristry judges. Their role is to answer any competitor's questions before the competition, and then once the competition is under way to monitor for any violations and infringements of the rules of the competition.

These infringements can be:

- Over the size limitation.
- Late arrival for the start of the competition.
- Continuing to work when the competition time has ended.
- Using materials that are forbidden in the rules of the competition.
- Before the competition constructing any elements of the design that have been expressly prohibited.
- Assistants can also incur penalty points for their designer if they do not leave a designated area on time or if they place horticultural materials into the design, unless it is specifically acceptable in the rules of the competition to do so.
- Interference with another contestants work would generally mean instant disqualification.

Penalty points

If the judge or technical committee find any violations of the competition rules then they may award penalty points, and these will be on a sliding scale depending on the degree of infringement. Minor discrepancies means only a few points will be lost whilst blatant breaches can result in deductions of ten points or more per judge.

In international competitions the contestants are not always notified of point deductions.

Aide Memoire

Often for larger competitions, i.e. 'The Florist of the Year competition,' you will be given an aide memoire that lays out the rules of the competition.

An aide memoire is a document that lists everything a competitor needs to know about the competition. It is compiled to help contestants understand the rules of the competition, all the information needed to compete such as the domestic arrangements, i.e. accommodation etc., the competition schedules and much more will be found in it.

An aide memoire will consist of:

- The rules of the competition.
- The competition schedules.
- The venue. This will include the name and address of the venue and any hall number.
- A timetable. This is invaluable as it shows where the competitor must be at any given time and when the competitions start and end.
- Accommodation. This will give the name and address of hotels etc., and the dates that the organisers will be paying for, if any.
- A marking scheme.
- Judging facets.
- Competitor's assistant. If an assistant is allowed the rules governing their role will be explained.
- Judging. This will clarify how many judges there will be and the judging procedure.
- Health and Safety issues.
- Rules for questions and answers. Questions are allowed and will be answered by a technical committee, generally there is a cut off time for questions.

The wording of the schedule holds clues to what the judge is looking for.

Generally in floristry competitions the wording 'Fresh flowers and plant material must predominate,' are included in most schedules. The flowers and foliage should tell the story and portray the schedules meaning. Accessories used within the design such as, pins, fabric, beads etc. should never dominate.

'The judges will be looking for a high standard of design and technical skills,' is another sentence used as a reminder to competitors that shoddy work will not win prizes.

Tips

- Read the schedule carefully
- Strip down the words weighing the implications of each one.
- Consider the mark schedule, look at the facets and think about them against the written schedule.
- Look at the marking facets and decide where the most marks can be gained.
- Think out the types of design you could make within the boundaries of the schedules.
- Abide by the rules.

Chapter 6:
How to understand what the judge is looking for

❝ A single moment of understanding can flood a whole life with meaning. ❞
Anon

In this chapter:
- What makes a florist a floral designer?
- Understanding the design techniques
- Idea
- Colour and colour wheel
- Composition
- Technique
- Conclusion

The judge of the day will have done their homework and will have studied the schedule in much the same way as the competitors have done. They will have analysed all the words and studied the schedule of marking facets. They will arrive with an open mind ready to find the winner. Inexperienced competitors may think that a particular judge likes a specific colour harmony or style of design. This is simply not true; in the competition room judging is performed to a set of universal standards whereby the judge can see whether an exhibit has met the criteria of artistic and technical merit. Personal preference will not come into any floristry judges' decisions.

Floristry judges are always approachable, but the judge of the day will sit quietly out of the way whilst competition entries are staged. This is not because they are aloof; it is simply that they do not wish to see any competition entries before they start judging. Floristry judges are there to help competitors and they will always find time to talk after the competition.

What makes a florist a floral designer?

Floristry generally has to be functional, a bridal bouquet must be made so that it can be carried, a headdress so that it can be worn, a funeral tribute must be emotive to convey a sentiment, each piece suitable for its purpose. Manual dexterity is essential and a florist has these skills; a floral designer goes beyond these abilities to express feelings and gather an emotional response from the onlooker, receiver or judge.

Designs made by floral artists will reach out and touch the feelings, capture an uplifting connection, a dynamic 'take your breath away' reaction. Think back to the time you saw a floristry design that blew your mind by its inherent beauty and meaning; it remains in the memory forever.

This is the true floral artist who will have identified and elevated their designs through an understanding of the materials they work with and the techniques of design they apply. They are passionate about their work and it shines through in their designs.

Understanding the design techniques.

> *Life is not measured by the number of breaths we take, but by the moments that take our breath away.*
> *Anon*

The principles and elements of design have been the fundamental visual values that have been used for centuries to determine whether artwork is perceived as good. These rules are applied to all competition work throughout the floristry world. In some countries the interpretation might differ slightly, but the basic principles will remain. Therefore competitors would be foolish to ignore these rules. Understanding and applying these guidelines will result in a well-organised design.

It is imperative that a well thought out idea is formed before starting on a competition piece, without this the design will be confusing and haphazard. Studying the principles and elements of design will help competitors' to understand what the judge is looking for. The winning entry will have had a carefully crafted plan.

There are four groups of marks that judges apply to every competition piece, each set relating to an aspect of design or technique. The judge will deduct marks from each category for faults and mistakes and they will be able to tell you, at the end of the competition, where you have lost points. The facets are:

IDEA
COLOUR
COMPOSITION
TECHNIQUE

Within these sets of marks are other factors that help the judge determine what is good about a competition entry.

This is an example of a marking scheme. However this changes from time to time, depending on the competition.

		Max. Mark
Idea: (Distinction)	Originality, Uniqueness, Creativity. Interpretation. Choice of and design with materials.	20
TOTAL FOR IDEA		**20**
Colour:	Proportion/dominance of colours used, expression of idea in colours, colour-composition (contrasts, harmony, value of colours etc), placement of colours	20
TOTAL FOR COLOUR		**20**
Composition:	Shape/Style/Form/Texture/Contrasts	10
	Movement/Rhythm/Volume/ Dominance	10
	Proportion/Visual Balance/Harmony/ Line/Use of Space	10
TOTAL FOR COMPOSITION		**30**
Technique: (Workmanship)	Condition of materials. Guarantee of durability.	
	Method of construction	10
	Finish and workmanship.	10
	Stability of work/actual (physical) balance, suitability of technique	10
TOTAL FOR TECHNIQUE		**30**
Total Marks		**100**

Idea

This section of marks deals with the original idea, the inspiration behind the concept. This is the creativity, unique vision and imagination plus expression of feeling that will go into the work to elevate it above the other competition pieces. It's giving the work distinction.

Distinction the dictionary definition:
'That which arrests the beholder.'

It means there are special characteristics or excellence within the design. It could be the original use of ordinary materials, a clever concept, an original idea, simply perfection in a classic design, or a meaningful expression of the theme.

There are also marks for how all the materials, flowers and foliage have been chosen and used to carry the idea through with clarity of design to a successful, complete, competition piece.

Also in this category is 'Interpretation.' This is the way the completed design translates the wording of the schedule with the use of flowers and plant material. The design should reach out and immediately affirm the theme of the competition. Accessories should not be necessary; the flowers and plant material and design of the work should portray the meaning to the judge.

Colour

Choosing innovative colour harmonies is an artistic skill of its own. The facets within the colour section help the judge to determine the degree of expertise a competitor has used to create a well-balanced colour scheme.

The way that colour is distributed will affect the proportion and visual balance of the whole design. The creation of areas of heightened colour - dominance - will add colour interest and impact. The use of shades, tints and tones of colours will give added degrees of richness and/or subtlety to the chosen colour scheme, and provide clever transition from one colour to another. Without contrasts of colour the design may become dull. Where colours are placed and how they are linked to each other will have an enormous effect on the visual harmony of the design.

Expression of idea in colour means using a colour harmony to convey the theme of the schedule. Colour is emotive; it can be exhilarating or passive, capture a mood, show a personality or be reminiscent of a country.
Colour is a powerful tool, study the colour wheel and applying its principles imaginatively will help get a good overall mark for colour.

Studying the colour wheel and applying it in everyday work will help when choosing colour schemes for competitive work.

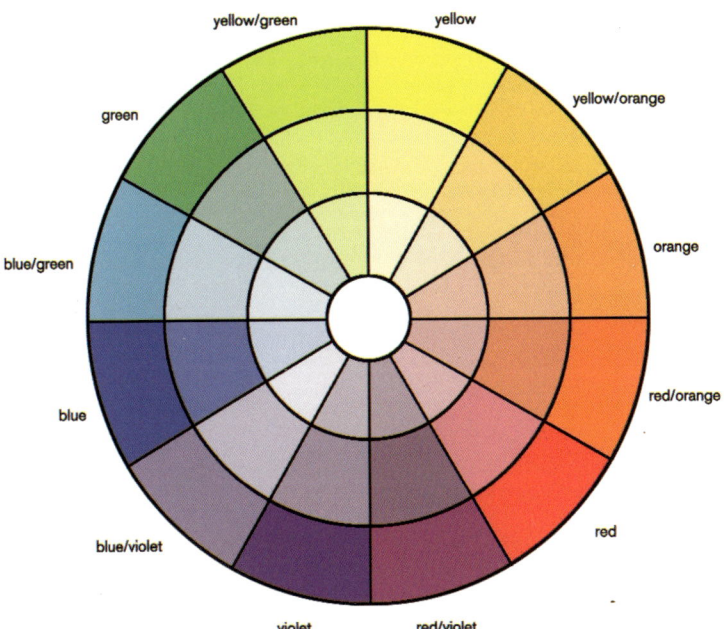

Composition

This section concerns how to choose and use your selected materials, and the way the design is planned and organised to give maximum visual appeal. It is the result of a carefully thought out plan using form, shape, texture and contrasts to produce a harmonious finished design.

There must be strength of style, artistic unity means staying with the style you have chosen without adding other distracting elements. Too many forms within the design will be confusing; too little will be monotonous, a good balance will give a clear style statement.

Texture is the tangible, feely, touchy, surface quality that will give depth and substance to a design. Texture is a strong element that is essential, particularly when making a design in only one colour; it can dramatically change the effect of a competition piece. Texture is both visual and actual.

Movement and Rhythm is needed to sustain interest and allow the eye to flow through the design in a series of motion and rest, it can be achieved by use of repetition and variety of forms. Spontaneous natural movement can be a powerful element in design.

Dominance means using bolder materials to create emphasis in some areas of the design, giving drama and power and a focus for the eye to rest.

Proportion and scale are closely allied and relate to size and the relationship of each element of the design, the space it occupies and its surroundings. There are formulas of proportion that can be seen in nature, the way plants grow, seed patterns etc., the Golden Section is one of these that has been used by artists for centuries. However there are numerous variations of these guidelines and the designer must choose how to interpret these.

How materials and colour are placed within the design will affect the visual balance. The design may look top heavy or about to fall over because of the position of flowers and foliage although it might not be unstable. Materials with strong visual weight if positioned incorrectly will make a design look unsteady and unbalanced.

Using space within a design will define and enhance the flowers and foliage used. The use of space will give clarity and definition to individual areas within the work.

Harmony will result when all the components come together to create a unified look, each part mixing effortlessly and seamlessly with each other within the design. Harmony is the sublime aspect that all designers aim for.

Technique

A competitor can gain maximum marks by using meticulous workmanship and perfect, well-conditioned flowers. The finish of the design must be flawlessly neat and crisp, no blobs of glue, frayed ribbon, damaged flowers or unsightly wiring. If containers are used these should look pristine and perfect.

The technique that is used to construct the design should be suitable for the type of work stated in the schedule. This is particularly important when creating bridal designs that have to be carried and therefore need careful consideration in construction.

The word 'condition' refers to the freshness of the flowers and plant material used. There should be no blemishes on any flower or leaf; they should be faultless in every way and at the peak of their perfection. Respecting the natural materials will give strength to a design.

The judge will be evaluating whether the flowers chosen will last through the occasion stated in the schedule, the materials durability for the event is essential.

The stability of the work and (actual or physical) balance means that the construction is firm, all the materials anchored well, and the mechanics secure. The design will not fall over or come to pieces because of technical faults. This is fundamental for every floristry item and competition piece, no matter what type of design; it must have a firm foundation to build on.

Conclusion

Clever floral designers stretch the elements and principles of design to their limit in the quest for a unique visionary design. However the design rules have to be learnt first before you can experiment and expand them, they are the building blocks to a winning design.

There are many books to study on the principles and elements of design but nature has the best design examples for florists and competitors. The design rules may seem difficult to understand at first, but examine nature, look at a flower growing, their form and patterns and before you will unfold all the principles and elements of good design. Nature is the best learning tool of all for every artist.

Chapter 7:
Design tips and common faults

"Creativity is allowing yourself to make mistakes. Design is knowing which ones to keep."
Scott Adams

In this chapter:
- General design tips
- Design shapes made simple
- How to gain more marks for colour
- Winning tips for bridal designs and body accessories
- Hand tied designs
- Flower arrangement tips
- Funeral tribute advice
- Planted design guidelines
- My own designs

This chapter will help you identify some of the common faults competitors make, plus giving design tips and hints to improve and upgrade skill levels. It's not an exhaustive list, and after the competition you will pick up valuable advice from the judge about your own personal design ability.

Record your marks and the judge's comments in the section at the end of this chapter; this will be a reminder not to make the same mistakes in the next competition. Also note any good features the judge has remarked on, so that you can build on these for the future. Keep your score cards for every competition and analyse them.

General design tips

- Read THE SCHEDULE CAREFULLY AND UNDERSTAND THE WORDING.
- Have a clear picture in your mind of the finished design. Draw the design if necessary. Place the drawing on your work bench to keep the image in focus.
- Use the elements of design. Form, Space, Colour, Texture. These are the building blocks to creating great designs.
- Think about the principles of design - every great artist uses them instinctively.
- Keep expanding and stretching your original concept, pushing the boundaries.
- Will the design chosen suit the theme of the competition schedule?
- Give your design feeling, an emotional message and connection, without the use of words.
- DO NOT OVER ACCESSORIZE. The flowers should relay the message.
- Only use drapes or accessories around your competition piece if the schedule asks for them. They will often detract from the competition entry.
- Do not use too many design ideas in one piece. Simplicity is often the key to winning.
- Know when to stop adding flowers and foliage. Restraint is the solution in good design.
- Don't be over ambitious; know what you can achieve in the time limit.
- Immaculate presentation will gain excellent marks.
- Decide on a colour scheme.
- Pay attention to technique and workmanship, the technical section is where you can gain maximum marks with meticulous work.
- What elements/materials will elevate your design above the rest of the competition entries.
- The judge will want to inspect your work thoroughly. Make sure the judge can handle the design easily. You could lose marks if the judge cannot remove your design for scrutiny.
- Nature has the best lessons; the way the flower grows will show you how to use it.

Design shapes made simple

In the mind there is often an excess of ideas and materials that will make design thoughts muddled. There are endless forms and colours to think about, and sometimes you need to think of a design shape quickly, particularly when you are making a surprise item. Focus and simplicity is the key if the head is whizzing with ideas or you cannot come up with a solution.
Think in terms of shapes to simplify the process.

What shape will it be?

Generally the design will be one of these shapes:

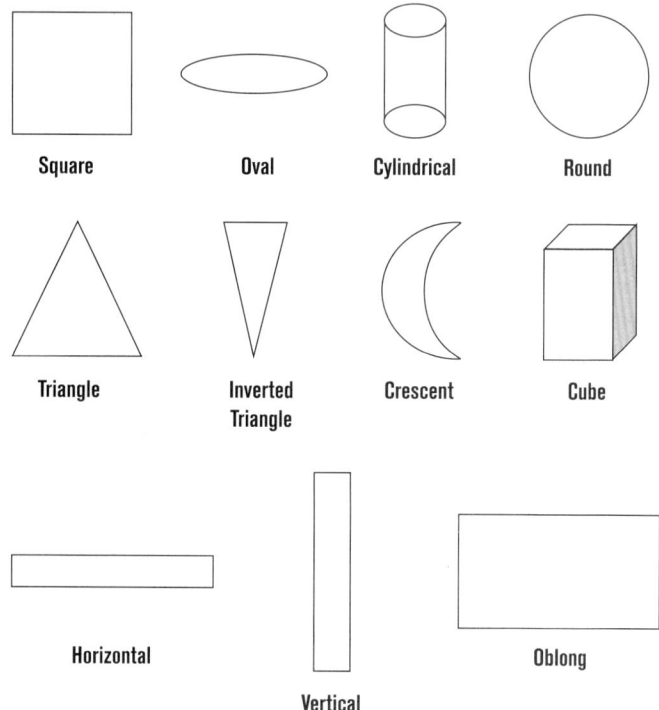

How to gain more marks for colour

- Think about how many shades of each differing colour you will use for a harmonious effect.
- Using equal amounts of bold colours is difficult and can be overpowering.
- A general guide when using three colours, choose, 70% of one, 20% of the second, 10% of third colour.
- Add visual interest with surface texture.
- Don't stick to just one colour; there should be tones, tints and shades to gain more colour points.
- Plan the colour scheme; take time to think about unusual harmonies.
- Multi coloured, polychromatic colours can be very difficult to use successfully, unless you are a skilled colourist.
- If you are not instinctively good with colour start to learn by using the colour wheel in shop work every day.
- Lime green is luminous and makes most colour harmonies zing.
- Darker tones give depth of colour, for example burgundy harmonizes with most other colours.
- Green and white - great if you use tints, tones and shade of each colour. Not if you use one hue of green and white, there needs to be light and shade in the colour harmony.
- For great combinations of colour, look at paint charts, interior décor brochures, art galleries, gardens and design exhibitions.

Winning tips for bridal designs and body accessories

- The comfort of the bride or wearer is paramount.
- For bridal designs to be carried there should be a clear method of how to hold the design.
- Handles on bridal bouquets should be light and soft to hold. There should be no abrasive materials or sharp objects to harm the bride.
- Bridal designs to be carried must be light in weight and carefully balanced they should be easy to hold in the hand or rest on the arm.
- Think about how the bridal piece will be held and design with this in mind. Often a bridal design looks totally different when held. Use a mirror to see the effect when the design is held.
- The back of the design should be finished off as perfectly as the front.

There should be something interesting and neat at the back for the bride to look at.

- Make sure all designs have a profile; they are viewed from the sides as well as the front.
- Before presenting for judging all headdresses or body accessories should be tried on, to ensure they are comfortable to wear.
- All bridal and body designs should be light in weight. Use the finest wires and materials possible.
- How will it be secured? There must be some method of securing any headdresses or accessories.
- Remember that delicate flowers in headdresses and accessories will wilt rapidly. Use sturdy flower material that will last well.
- Ensure flowers, foliage and all the materials will not stain garments.
- Consider the schedule, i.e., wedding, ball, prom etc., this will determine the style of the design.
- Consider the fit of body accessories, make the fastening adjustable where possible unless there are exact measurements for ankles, wrists etc.

Hand tied designs

Hand tied designs need expertise in technique, and each style will need a different construction method. The fundamental principles listed here always apply;

- All stems must be firmly tied.
- The back of the design must be finished off neatly.
- All stems should be cleaned and reach the water line.

If the hand tied design is to be presented in a container then there must be unity of design, flower material, and colour with the container.

Any framework must be an integral part of the design and finished neatly.

Tying techniques

When making hand tied designs there are a variety of tying techniques to choose from, and the method used will depend on the design.

Spiralling stems
This is the standard method used in hand tied designs to give an open look.

Parallel stems
Stems placed side by side in a straight line, suitable for linear designs and some presentation bouquets where a slimmer handle is required.

Structure technique
Using a base structure, i.e. grid, twig frame, wire ring etc. Generally the structure is made from pliable materials.

Hand tied bridal designs

Hand tied bridal bouquets need a different technique to other hand tied designs. Bridal hand tied bouquets have to be carried therefore the comfort of the holder must be considered:

- The biggest fault when making hand tied wedding designs is the 'closed umbrella' look where the design finishes way above the tie point, leaving an unsightly view of stems and foliage. Flowers and materials must graduate down to the tie point on circular/posy designs.
- Make sure hand tied designs have a profile.
- Collars and framework must be meticulously executed.
- The finish of the bouquet must be scrupulously neat.
- It is important too have a soft covering for ease of holding, where the stems are to be held on a hand tied bridal design. This should be devoid of sharp or abrasive materials.
- Tie stems firmly and neatly, don't forget that stems will lose moisture and shrink when they are left out of water, which may result in the binding coming loose, if not tied very tightly.
- Ensure the stems are clean and neat.
- The design is to be carried so should be light in weight.

Winning tips for floral arrangements

In floristry competitions flower arrangement covers a wide variety of designs, from large open choice floral compositions to small table arrangements, from freestanding structures to classic arrangements made in floral foam. Sometimes the schedule will dictate the style of design or occasion, i.e., table design.

The one fundamental principle is that all designs must be made on firm foundations and skill in construction is crucial.

Tips

- Build on a firm foundation first; it's no good creating a wonderful design that falls over.
- A variety of shapes and textures can add interest to the design.
- Use well conditioned fresh flowers and foliage.
- Determine the colour scheme.
- Don't clutter the design; emphasize the flowers with the use of space.
- Visual balance is one of the keys to good design. Develop an eye for good balance.
- Decide on the water source, i.e., floral foam, test tubes etc.
- Choose the technique of design first, for example, in a container, free standing without the support of a container etc.
- Make sure all flowers and plant materials are firmly anchored.
- Do not distract with two many clever design ideas in one arrangement.
- The container will be an integral part of the design unless otherwise stated in the schedule, choose wisely, for colour shape and style.
- Front facing designs must be finished neatly at the back.
- Use only top quality, well-conditioned flowers and foliage, blemishes mean lost marks.
- Consider whether the mechanics need concealing.
- Gift arrangement should have an easily accessible watering method.
- Don't copy designs made by others, try to bring a unique aspect to your own arrangement.

Funeral tributes

Floral funeral tributes are a major part of our industry so it is fitting that competition schedules incorporate these designs.

- Make sure the tribute has a profile, so that any unsightly base is covered.
- Always place the finished tribute on the floor and view from above.
- All flowers, foliage and materials must be firmly anchored into the base.
- The finish should be neat, no frayed ribbon, dirty moss or damaged plant material.
- Funeral tributes must be easy to handle, with no wires or sharp items to cause damage.
- Think about the principles of design and apply them to the tribute.
- If the tribute is to be transported it should be light in weight.
- A funeral tribute should be emotive and significant for the occasion or representative of the deceased.
- Only use the best quality flowers that have been well conditioned.
- If adding a message card ensure it is neatly written and all spellings are correct.

Planted designs

Planted design competitions need special attention. If possible a planted design should be made up a few days before the competition to allow the plants to bed in. However, this is not always possible particularly in a surprise competition.

There are different forms of planted design, whatever the style the principles of good design should be observed.

- Choose a suitable container, large enough to hold all the plants comfortably.
- Visual balance is extremely important in planted designs.
- All plants must be healthy, enjoy the same living conditions and be compatible with each other. For example, do not plant cacti with water loving plants as one or both will die rapidly.
- Whatever the medium used, i.e., soil, moss, compost, all plants must be firmly planted.
- The container must complement the plants in colour, texture, size and shape.
- If accessories are used they must enhance the design and be well anchored in.
- Good proportions are essential in planted designs.
- A variety of shapes, forms and textures can add interest to the design.
- Cover any unsightly soil with a decorative topping.
- Consider how the design will be watered without spillage.

My own designs

On these pages record your own marks and judges comments.

	Mark Given
IDEA:	
COLOUR:	
COMPOSITION:	
TECHNIQUE:	

Total Marks

Judges Comments:

	Mark Given
IDEA:	
COLOUR:	
COMPOSITION:	
TECHNIQUE:	

Total Marks

Judges Comments:

Chapter 7: Design tips and common faults

	Mark Given
IDEA:	
COLOUR:	
COMPOSITION:	
TECHNIQUE:	
Total Marks	

Judges Comments:

	Mark Given
IDEA:	
COLOUR:	
COMPOSITION:	
TECHNIQUE:	
Total Marks	

Judges Comments:

Chapter 8:
Surprise/Mystery competitions

> *Mystery is at the heart of creativity that, and surprise.*
> *Julia Cameron*

In this chapter:
- Practice makes perfect
- Open and closed judging
- Tips on how to win

Surprise or Mystery competitions are the most challenging type of floristry competitions. Competitors work with previously unseen materials and are given a timescale to complete the task. Generally time is allowed before the start of the competition to look at the flowers, foliage and sundries given and plan the design to be made. Competitors must have the ability to think on their feet, because the way the time allowed for planning is used is the key to success. Mental speed is essential to assimilate the information and quickly formulate a plan. Now is the time to trust your initial ideas, don't waste time dithering, be clear headed and go with the design. Relax and pace yourself throughout the competition.

Practice makes perfect

It's a good idea to practice several designs in your workroom, ideas that can be adjusted to fit any tasks given. It's easy to get a mental block when under pressure; by practising you already have a store of designs to pull out in an emergency.

The best advice is keep going with the design; if its not going according to plan, think about how to improve or tweak it. Don't abandon a design and start another half way through the competition, it can be the route to disaster. Relax, don't panic, think it through and run with it.

Open and closed judging

There are different ways in which floristry competitions are judged and the competitor should be aware of these and understand how they work. Closed judging is where the pieces are taken from the competitors to a judging room; the judge does not see the competitor or know whom they are. This type of judging is most common in England; although in Surprise competitions the judges may wander between the competitors whilst they are making their surprise items. More about open judging in Chapter 9 - Competing overseas.

Tips on how to win a surprise or mystery competition

There are different ways in which floristry competitions are judged and the competitor should be aware of these and understand how they work. Closed judging is where the pieces are taken from the competitors to a judging room; the judge does not see the competitor or know whom they are. This type of judging is most common in England; although in Surprise competitions the judges may wander between the competitors whilst they are making their surprise items. More about open judging in Chapter 9 - Competing overseas.

Tips

- READ THE SCHEDULE CAREFULLY.
- Identify the most important elements of the design to be made, i.e. if it's a bracelet how will it be worn, stability, construction etc.
- Take time to plan and focus on the materials given. Formulate the idea. Sketch the design if necessary; keep this image in your mind.
- Decide on a colour scheme.
- Look carefully at the flowers, foliage and plant material given to you, what do they say to you, how do they grow? Is there lots of trailing foliage, more round flowers, or line material? This will determine the sort of design you make.
- Can you use one of your practice ideas or elements of the design for the surprise competition?
- Don't try the impossible; know what you can accomplish in the timescale.
- Good use of time catapults you to the front.
- Break up the time, i.e. if the competition is 1½ hours, fifteen minutes for planning, thirty minutes for making a frame or structure, thirty minutes for adding flowers and foliage, fifteen minutes for checking, finishing and polishing the design. In this way you will never run out of time.
- Simplify the design process. Think what shape the finished design will be, make the decision before starting the work. If there is a structure to make think in terms of simple shapes, round, square, oblong etc.

- Practice mystery items before the competition, have one or two ideas that you can adapt to any sort of schedule.
- Make sure plant material predominates. You may be given lots of accessories, use these with care. They should not detract from the flowers and foliage.
- Don't change your mind half way through. Go with the original idea, stick with it, and work it out.
- Don't look at what other competitors are doing, don't be influenced by them, they may be getting it wrong.
- Think where the water source will be, test tubes, floral foam etc?
- Never try something you have not practised or made before. A surprise competition is not the place to experiment in unknown areas.
- If making a framework then this should complement the flowers.
- Natural. unobtrusive materials are often best for structures.
- Don't use too many design ideas in one piece of work. Keep it simple.
- Pay attention to finish and neatness; make sure your work is technically perfect.
- Don't panic halfway through the competition; keep calm, focused, think it through. Never give in, keep going.
- KNOW WHEN TO STOP ADDING MATERIALS. If you have time left and the design is finished, don't make the mistake of adding more.

Chapter 9:
Competing overseas

" Even as a fierce competitor I try to smile. "
Magic Johnson

In this chapter:
- Aide Memoire
- Open judging
- After the competition

If you are asked to compete or represent your country in an overseas competition then you have reached the peak of competing. It's an honour bestowed to few competitors and with the accolade comes responsibility. For a start it's mind blowing and stressful to have the hopes of your country resting on your shoulders.

Before you leave your own country there are months of planning and preparation, six months minimum for a European or World competition, often longer. The commitment is huge and must never be underestimated. The competitor must make adequate arrangements within their workplace to allow for time to practice and space to think and prepare.

Generally a competitor will have an assistant designer to help at the competition and a manager to take away the responsibility of the paperwork and budget. There is still a colossal amount of work to do by the designer.

Aide Memoire

There will be an aide memoire from the organizing country and any questions can be addressed to the technical committee. All questions and answers asked by every competitor should be available for all to see.

There will also be a strict timetable to adhere to and it is inconsiderate to hold up any competitors meetings or proceedings by arriving late. The competition will not be held up for one competitor.

Try to get to the country a few days before the competition to familiarize yourself with the surroundings and venue. Also remember there may be time differences, so jet lag could be a problem.

Dress appropriately, other countries may have a dress code and adherence to this is important. There may also be a stage show, so take suitable smart clothes.

The competitor is an ambassador for their country and as such should uphold a harmonious relationship with the host and competing countries. It may be a fiercely fought competition, but a polite smiling demeanour will work wonders.

Open judging

In many world floristry competitions open judging takes place, and it is necessary for the competitor to understand how this works, and the reasons for this type of judging.

Open judging is when floristry judges walk freely amongst the competitors whilst they are making their entries. The judge marks the work as it is being made and they can come up to the competitor's bench to scrutinize the assembly technique. It can be quite daunting for competitors who are not used to this type of judging to have someone peering over their shoulder; but if the work is being perfectly made then the judge has the chance to evaluate the construction in more depth, therefore giving higher marks. If the work is neat and clever the competitor has nothing to hide, and the advantages of the judge seeing the assembly technique is of benefit to them. Alternatively if the work is shoddy the judge will immediately pick up on this and mark accordingly.

Floristry judges are trained to be professional, impartial and objective; it does not matter whether the competitor is known to the judge or not, the only consideration for the judge is the quality of the competitors work in front of them. Marking is done purely on the facets of design and technique. Competitors should not fear open judging, it is used in most other types of performance-based competitions in different subjects. There is more about open judging in Chapter 20.

After the competition

The competitor must also understand that after the competition there will be a period of readjustment before getting back into a normal routine. After months of solely focusing on the competition deflation is always going to occur and a way of relaxation will be needed. There is more about after the competition in Chapter 10.

This will be a unique experience and one that should be enjoyed, with a smile, to the full.

Chapter 10:
After the competition

"Win as if you were used to it, lose as if you enjoyed it for a change."
Ralph Waldo Emerson

In this chapter:
- After competition tips
- How to be a good winner
- How to be a good loser

There are some world floristry competitions that can take over a competitor's life for six to twelve months. These competitions are extremely hard work and result in nonstop pressure, where the competitor lives in a bubble of practice and continuous focus on the tasks of the competition. It's a relief when the competition day finally arrives and the entire practice comes into fruition. In the case of major competitions, there will be preparation days at the venue and then the tasks will be held over a number of days, with only the top scoring contestants going through to a live stage final.

After such a competition, the competitor will feel drained both physically and emotionally, and the after stress can cause major problems if there is not a proper period of adjustment. It is unsettling to come back down to reality and mundane work after such an exciting experience. Whether you are the winner or not, you will be tired out mentally and there will need to be a gentle climb down to normality. After the competition there should be an eagerness to return to the competition arena and not burn out and exhaustion.

After the competition tips

- Take time out to relax, a short holiday or a day out with friends.
- Eat well, get plenty of sleep and have some physical activity.
- Don't beat yourself up with 'what if's,' acknowledge where you could have done better, analyse and then move on.
- Review the competition and focus on what you did well.
- Mentally enjoy the positive aspects of the competition, the friendships gained; the fun of competing and take pride in knowing you did your personal best.

How to be a good winner

Winning is the ultimate goal, it is exhilarating, fun and glamourous, and can never be underestimated; after all that preparation, enjoy the ecstasy of achieving the highest accolade. Winning, however, is not without stress. Being the winner adds additional pressure and it is easy to let this award go to your head. Obviously there will be celebrations for you and your team of supporters, this is right and proper after all the hard work, but the winner should always be humble and gracious in victory. Showing off, being patronising or gloating have no part of winning and 'There by the grace of God go I,' is the attitude to adopt towards the losers.

Be a great winner, keep your friends and earn the respect of your opponents and colleagues with your magnanimous approach to winning.

The climb down to normality may be even harder for the winner of the competition. Days of relaxation and adjustment are essential, so the after competition tips are even more important in the days following the competition.

How to be a good loser

> *Every calamity is a spur and valuable hint.*
> **Ralph Waldo Emerson**

No one wants to lose, but there can only be one winner in a floristry competition. If you don't win how you conduct yourself, with good manners and dignity, will say a lot about the person you are. Obviously there will be a measure of disappointment, but this can be turned into a positive experience. Never argue with officials or the judge. The judge's decision is final. You can get valuable feedback about your design from talking to the judge who will be keen to pass on wise advice and encouraging comments. Be happy that you have taken up the challenge, trying and losing is far better than never trying at all. And you will have learnt an enormous amount about yourself and your floristry abilities from the competition experience. Have the courage to continue competing and one day it could be you with the first prize.

- Be gracious in defeat.
- Never argue with officials or the judge.
- Always congratulate the winner.
- Have the self-confidence to acknowledge the winning exhibits superiority.
- Analyse why the winning exhibit has come first, compared to the other entries.
- Acknowledge the fact that you might not have put enough time and practice into your entry.
- Talk to the judge who will explain where points have been gained and lost, listen carefully and absorb what they have to say.
- Learn from your mistakes, put them right and enter the next competition knowing that these faults will be rectified.
- Devise a training programme, ready for the next competition.
- Be happy that you have entered the competition and gained valuable experience.
- The judge's decision is final.

FOR JUDGES

Chapter 11:
What is a floristry judge?

“ To judge wisely, we must know how things appear to the unwise. ”
George Eliot

In this chapter:
- How to become a floristry judge
- The qualities of a good floristry judge
- Training to be a judge
- Continuous professional development

A floristry judge is an authorized florist who is appointed to decide the winners at a floristry competition. The judge evaluates floristry competition exhibits based on recognised standards of design and technique and then forms a judgment after careful consideration of these standards. A floristry judge at all times upholds and maintains the high standards set in floristry judging.

How to become a floristry judge.

Floristry judging is rewarding, time consuming and requires dedication to the craft of floristry. To enable you to become a floristry judge you must be an experienced florist with both practical and theoretical knowledge of floristry, art and design.

To attain the necessary knowledge to become a floristry judge generally more than ten years floristry experience is required. Knowledge of floristry competitions and how they are run is a benefit; being a successful competitor is sometimes an advantage. Although this will not necessarily make you a good judge, as often great competitors/designers only view others work from their own perspective, without considering the broader viewpoint.

Examine your motives about becoming a floristry judge. Floristry judging is not done for glory or status. There has to be generosity of spirit and a definite willingness to impart floristry knowledge, together with enthusiasm for helping floristry competitors achieve greater goals. A floristry judge must have common sense, a clear and coherent mind, and a degree of analytical prowess.
Above all a floristry judge must be capable of making independent, impartial, consistent decisions. They must have the temperament, tact, diplomacy and personality to overcome difficult situations in the competition room. A judge always acts with tolerance, kindness and a degree of firmness, thus gaining the respect of their peers. A floristry judge must have the ability to express themselves confidently in writing and verbally both individually with feedback to competitors and to a wider audience.

smart, modern, professional appearance is essential for a floristry judge.

The qualities of a good floristry judge

- A floristry judge must be diligent, committed and reliable.
- Have an organised, coherent mind.
- The ability to make independent decisions.
- A great knowledge of floristry and allied subjects.
- Wide understanding of the principles and elements of design.
- A good knowledge of flowers, foliage and plant material.
- Be able to judge impartially, without favouritism.
- To be fair and honest and at all times act with integrity.
- To have a sincere desire to be of service to floristry competitions.
- The temperament and personality to handle stressful situations.
- Have the capabilities to validate any judging decisions verbally and confidently in feedback to competitors.
- To speak clearly, confidently and concisely to an audience.
- To look smart and professional whilst on judging assignments.
- Make the time to continually expand knowledge of new techniques and styles.
- Try to attend as many floristry competitions as possible even when not judging.
- To maintain a united judging policy, never criticizing another judge, a judgement or schedule.
- Never express a personal preference, feedback is always based on judging facts.
- Be able to write coherent and concise competition schedules.
- Always acting in a manner that earns respect and gives credibility to floristry judges.
- To evaluate competition entries and mark carefully and consistently.
- To have a keen sense of discernment, perceiving quickly between good, mediocre and bad.
- To uphold and maintain the national floristry judging standards.

Training to be a judge

There will be a period of training for all floristry judges generally culminating in a practical and written examination. Often there is a period of internship where shadow judging will take place generally with a mentor judge. Stewarding competitions will give prospective judges an insight into the competition room.

Continuous professional development

Even for qualified floristry judges there is continuous professional development. Floristry judges must be abreast of new techniques and design styles together with a wide knowledge of flower and plant varieties. There is always something new to learn, floristry judging is a constant challenge and not for the faint hearted.

Above all to become a floristry judge there has to be a sincere desire to be of service to floristry, and a dedication to the pursuit of excellence in the competition room.

Chapter 12:
The judges code of conduct

> " Excellence calls for character ....integrity ...fairness ...honesty ... a determination to do what's right. High ethical standards, across the board. "
>
> *Price Pritchett*

In this chapter:
- Judges code of ethics
- Judging criteria

Floristry judges are at the forefront of the floral industry and how judges behave, both in the competition room and beyond, will reflect on the credibility of all floristry judges and their organizations.

Most judging associations and guilds will have their own code of conduct and ethics; these will be based on respect, loyalty, honesty and integrity. There has to be a shared commitment to each other, a united respect and reliability both whilst judging competitions and in a private capacity away from the judging room. Loyalty to other judges is paramount. Often an innocuous remark made by a judge can be blown out of all proportion and a moment of thought before speaking can avert complications arising. NEVER discuss or undermine a judging decision. Floristry judges have a duty to support fellow judges.

Floristry judges generally try to avoid knowing the competitors names, although this is not always possible in international competitions where there is open judging. There should always be a declaration of interest if a judge personally knows a competitor. If there is a competitor who works in a judge's business then it would be unethical to judge that particular competition. The integrity of floristry judges must be upheld at all times.

It is unwise to judge too many competition entries at one time. Up to twenty four are acceptable, any more would need an additional judge. Competition organisers should know in advance how many entries they would be having, although one or two competition entries may arrive on the day without prior notice.

Generally the written competition schedules have been well thought out in advance, and should have gone through a rigorous assessment by a number of floristry judges. Publicly or privately criticising schedules is not the remit of the judge. Any disagreements with the schedule should be taken up in writing with the judging association.

This is the code of ethics of the UK Floristry Judges Guild.

Judges' code of ethics

- It is the Judges responsibility to arrive punctually and allow plenty of time after general commentary for private comments.
- To study the schedule carefully, analysing the words before the competition.
- To judge every piece - only disqualifying any piece showing obvious disregard to the schedule, and even then to mark any which have to be disqualified. These marks will not count.
- Never to criticise another Judge - or their judgement. This should apply to both public commentary and private comments with competitors or other florists.
- When attending a competition in a private capacity, a qualified Judge must guard against being drawn into an expression of opinion, which could be contrary to that of the Judge, or Judges appointed for the occasion.
- LOYALTY BETWEEN JUDGES IS ESSENTIAL.
- Never to single out obviously poor floristry publicly. The Judges job is to find the winner, not to discourage the beginner.
- Keep any criticism of the schedule to a judges support day.
- It is not ethical for a Judge to know who the competitors are, or from which shop the entries came. The steward and judge should make every effort to see that there is nothing to identify the entries.
- Placing and marks must be checked with the steward before the winners are announced.
- Judges may not enter local or national floristry competitions.
- To obtain competitors names from the stewards before leaving the meeting and to send in named mark sheets promptly to UK Judges Guild after the competition.
- At all times seeking to enhance the profile of the UK Floristry Judges' Guild.
- THE JUDGES DECISION IS FINAL.

Judging criteria

There is often a further set of standards that floristry judges abide by, and competition entries are judged by. These are generally drawn up by the floristry judging association a judge belongs to; for example, these rules may state how a competition should be judged or the preparation that a judge should make before the competition. These standards may vary between countries and judging associations

This is the judging criterion of the UK Floristry Judges Guild.

Regardless of what floristry competition a competitor enters, all judges from the UK Floristry Judges Guild use the following principles of evaluation.

- To read and interpret the intentions of a schedule, understand the words used and emotion involved.
- Enter the competition room with an open mind receptive to all interpretations of the schedule.
- To appreciate and understand a wide range of floristry and connected subjects, and to understand the principles and elements of good design.
- To judge fairly the elements of idea, colour, composition, and technique and the facets within each category.
- To mark consistently and impartially between one design and another.
- To recognise a wide variety of flower and plant material.
- To assess accurately the quality and condition of the flower and plant material used.
- To observe accurately, recognising the merits and distinguishing between major faults and minor carelessness in each design.
- To be decisive and impersonal in judgement.
- To express any of the above both in writing and in speech. To justify a mark or a decision made confidently and eloquently, so that the Judges authority can be respected.
- To speak in public with confidence, authority, assurance and ease.
- To use designs from competitions to teach and encourage competitors and florists, helping to achieve a higher standard of professional floristry.
- To help observing trainee judges understand the judging process.
- At all times seeking to enhance the profile of the UK Floristry Judges Guild.

Chapter 13:
Judges training

" Information is pretty thin stuff unless mixed with experience. "
Clarence Day

In this chapter:
- Practical sessions
- Continuous professional development
- Shadow judging

Trainee judges are generally expected to attend a series of seminars designed to enhance judging skills and techniques. The seminars take the form of talks and discussions plus practical evaluation and marking exercises. Often an experienced judge or distinguished orator will be invited to attend and will give their views on some aspect of judging, commentaries or personal preparation.

Practical sessions

In the practical sessions there will be a series of marking exercises to establish mark levels, train the eye and develop discernment. A trainee judge would be expected to support any judging decisions with clear concise reasons given verbally, and would also be asked to give a commentary at some sessions. All these exercises are designed as confidence builders and preparation for judging assignments.

Generally trainee judges are evaluated at each seminar, and some people may decide after the first session that judging is not for them; alternatively some may not be invited to continue. Judging is not for everyone and it may be that other skills will be more dominant.

Shadow judging is a great way to learn the practicalities of judging and this is an important part of a judges training. (More about shadow judging later.)

At the end of the training, which generally takes approximately two years, there is sometimes a written and practical examination.

At all times trainee judges must adhere to the Judges code of Ethics and criteria laid down by their judging organisation.

Continuous professional development

Once trained, judges undergo continuous professional development, and essential judges support days and training are generally mandatory. Also judges must continue to keep updated with design styles and techniques, visiting floristry competitions, demonstrations and events whenever possible to continue professional growth.

Shadow judging

> *Follow then the shining ones, the wise, the awakened, the loving, for they know how to work and forbear.*
> **Buddha**

Shadow judging is an important way to develop the skills necessary to become a floristry judge. A trainee judge will not take part in the actual marking of the competition, although they may mark the competition independently to see how their marks compare to the judge's.

All decision-making will be taken by the judge of the day. If time allows the judge may discuss the marks given with the trainee judge and the judge may also be asked, on some occasions, to fill in an evaluation sheet on the trainee judge's performance.

It is an honour to be a trainee judge. To be allowed into the competition room whilst judging takes place is a privilege. Any views expressed by the judge in the competition room must never be commented on outside the judging room by the trainee judge. Confidentiality and loyalty to other judges is essential. Neither must trainee judges express any opinions to competitors or others at the competition. Only the judge of the day talks to competitors, although the trainee judge would be wise to listen to any discussions and the judge's commentary to gain valuable knowledge.

A trainee judge must always arrive early to ensure there is time for a discussion with the judge of the day, before marking takes place.

Shadow judging is one of the most valuable exercises; here the trainee judge learns first hand how judges conduct themselves in the competition room and beyond.

Chapter 14:
How to prepare for a judging assignment

In all things, success depends upon previous preparation, and without such preparation there is sure to be failure. **Confucius**

In this chapter:
- Check all information
- Reading the schedules
- Essential judging kit
- At the venue

When asked to judge a competition it is imperative that you check you are available, and then reply promptly. Invitations to judge are generally made a long time in advance so think carefully before taking a judges assignment, make sure no other events or workplace commitments will prohibit you from attending. Once you have affirmed, it is unprofessional to cancel at short notice unless it is due to extreme extenuating circumstances.

Check you have all the information you need.

- Date and time of competition
- Location of competition
- Competition schedule and marking forms
- Contact numbers of organiser and venue (in case of emergency)

Travelling to the competition

When you travel will depend on the distance to the location. It maybe that overnight accommodation is required or flights need to be booked. This should be done well in advance to obtain the best value. It is vital that enough time is allowed for travel and to allow for any delays that might occur. Punctuality is also essential to produce a calm, stress free mental start to the judging and to give the organisers' time to introduce you. Arriving late flustered and hurried may result in a lack of concentration and an unprofessional appearance.

Generally the organiser will contact you the week before the competition to check travel plans and arrival time. If they do not, then a quick call to them will put your mind at rest.

A professional appearance

When on an assignment a floristry judge is the representative of all the floristry judges; how you conduct yourself and how you look will be a reflection on all judges. A professional, well-groomed, business look and manner is essential. A floristry judge should look calm, confident and in control at all times.

Remember that judging might be taking place in venues where climate temperatures vary. It can be very hot in hotels, or with air conditioning on, quite chilly. You may be judging in a marquee, where boots will be needed to get to the venue and an extra pair of shoes required. Be prepared for all weather conditions and eventualities.

Never leave the competition venue to early, make sure that flights and travel arrangements leave plenty of time to enable you to talk to the competitors after the competition.

Reading the schedules

Reading the schedules before the competition is an important part of a judge's preparation. Analyse the wording and marking facets. Write down any key points; think about any controversial issues that might arise, and generally prepare mentally for the judging task, this should be the norm before a competition. A judge should arrive without any pre-conceived ideas. Never underestimate the competitors.

Essential judging kit

Many floristry judges keep a 'judging briefcase' and in this are all the essentials needed for judging a competition.

- Pencils and sharpener
- Pen
- Rubber
- Clipboard
- Tape measure
- Spare paper to write your commentary on if necessary.
- Spare marking sheets
- A dictionary
- A watch
- Calculator
- A list of all the judges' names, addresses, e mail addresses and phone numbers, both land line and mobile phones.
(In case of emergencies.)

Always take the written competition schedule with you and marking facets. A copy of the Floristry Competitions book and any other small reference books that might be needed, these will help you should a query or complication arise. Don't assume there will be marking sheets available unless the organiser gives them to you in advance. It is far better to arrive with everything you need rather than worry on arrival that the necessary documents will not be provided.

At the venue

On arrival at the competition venue, introduce yourself to the organiser and then keep well out of the way. Competitors will be bringing in their entries and any judges should not see these until entry into the competition room. There should be no contact with competitors in the run up to the competition. Any questions asked by the competitors before the competition must be directed to the organiser or a technical committee. Competitors can misread any small talk you may have, however innocent with other competitors. Avoidance of competitors is essential until after the results have been announced.

Chapter 15:
Awarding marks

" Experience tells you what to do; confidence allows you to do it. "
Stan Smith

In this chapter:
- A fine balancing act
- Marks out of ten
- Who will be the winner?
- Marking sheets
- Respect of plant material
- Finding the winner

The judge's role is to allocate marks to competition entries based on fairness, honesty, knowledge and value. Discernment is perhaps the most important attribute for a judge. Having the skill to differentiate between good and bad aspects of design and techniques are pre-requisites. To be able to compartmentalise facets, appreciate and appraise exhibits, based on logical evaluation of the marking facets. There will always be an individual approach to judging, but personal preferences must be overcome as these will blight a judge's decisions and result in a lack of credibility.

An open mind, receptive to all concepts and with no preconceived ideas is needed to make suitable judgements. Impartiality is essential, with no allegiance to a particular style of design or colour. Nothing in the competition room should faze the judge in the quest to find the winner.

A fine balancing act

Sometimes a judge will find a competition entry that is totally revolutionary or perhaps a technique that is radical. A judge cannot be swayed because a design is ground breaking, just because it is new does not mean it has to be good, the same rigorous process of weighing the merits and faults of the design must take place. In the same vein a traditional design can be visually impaired, made incorrectly, or is not creative. It's a fine balancing act of standardising the level of marks and the marking sheet helps to break down the marks into manageable facets, enabling judges' to make accurate decisions.

The first quiet walk around the exhibits will help to set a mark level and experienced judges will already have some idea of outstanding or poor entries and an overall marking level. Whilst a judge's marks should never demoralise a competitor, they have to be fair, and being too kind with marks will be to the detriment of the competition. Again a fair balance must be achieved.

Be objective, decide what marks should be taken off for certain faults and if there are several entries with the same fault then this should show in a consistent level of marks. Developing a high degree of discernment is particularly important in higher skill level competitions. Always question yourself when awarding very high or low marks. Very little is absolutely perfect; nothing is totally without some merit. This is the time to have real clarity of judgement.

As a general guide always go back to check if a design has over a ninety mark, similarly with a mark below fifty-five.

This mark chart is a guideline only.

Marks out of 10

10 marks	✔	Perfect in every way – very rarely achieved
9 marks	✔	Almost perfection, one or two very minor faults
8 marks	✔	Very good
7 marks	✔	Good
6 marks	–	Satisfactory/Mediocre
5 marks	✘	Unsatisfactory
4 Marks	✘	Inadequate
3 marks	✘	Poor
2 marks	✘	Very poor
1 mark	✘	Unacceptable

Good discernment means that the judge uses a whole range of marks. One or two marks to distinguish between the first exhibit and the last one show poor discernment and a lack of confidence.

Fear of not making the popular choice puts pressure on the judge, but the judge is the only person who has inspected the entries thoroughly and can make a sound judgement, be true to yourself, confident in your knowledge.

Who will be the winner?

How will the judge decide what level of artistry is in a competition piece, what elevates one competitor's design above another? What makes it transcend from just a good floristry item to an art creation by a master designer? The judge must feel, think, consider and understand, its not just about using the principles and elements of design to evaluate, but recognising the added emotional ingredient that makes a design truly great. Only when a judge has observed art in all its manifestations will they be able to appreciate accurately what is presented for floristry judging at a higher-level competition. The design that lifts the heart will be the winner artistically. Read Chapter 6, 'How to understand what the judge is looking for' in conjunction with this chapter.

Marking sheets

A good marking sheet should be clear and easy to use. With enough space to add comments and marks against the competitor's exhibit number. It's worth considering using a spreadsheet on a laptop if facilities will allow. An example of a mark sheet is below.

Competitor No:	Idea (20)	Colour (20)	Composition (30) (10) (10) (10)	Technique (30) (10) (10) (10)	Total Marks	Place	Notes

Always ask to see the organisers mark sheet before the competition date, it may not be comfortable for you to use and you may want to make your own in advance and then transcribe the marks onto the official mark sheet. Care must be taken here though as most mistakes occur when copying from one to another sheet. Get the steward to help check and verify marks.

To recap the perfect design should have: -

a) Inherent beauty of design
b) An abundance of technical skill
c) A unique quality
d) Expressive use of colour
e) Clarity of meaning, tells a story or evokes an emotion
f) Respect for the natural beauty of plant material
g) Be functional for the intended use

Respect

Respect for plant material is a word that is often used in Europe in the marking facets, but is not widely used in Great Britain. It's the esteem in which the competitor holds the natural materials used. Respect is taking into consideration the natural beauty of the plant material without over manipulation or interference, showing an appreciation for the flowers, foliage and plant material. Respect is not often used in schedules for bridal design, accessories etc., where some manipulation is necessary.

Finding the winner

It's a relief for a floristry judge if there is a clear-cut winner in the competition, one outstanding design that elevates it to first prize. Often though this is not the case, and there may be two exceptional entries vying for first place. Similarly there may be several mediocre contenders that have similar marks coming into second place. This is when the judge is challenged and really has to concentrate, using all the powers and tools at their disposal to distinguish between the entries. Re-examination and evaluation is essential.

A fast decision may be necessary and this is where panic could set in. Panic is detrimental to decision making. Walk away for a few moments to clear the mind. Then return ask yourself this question;

"Why do these two entries have the same marks?"

This simple question sometimes is all that is needed to make the decision blindingly clear. Keep to a concentrated structure, think about the perfect design list on page 64, look at the facets again, and compare the marks given, then adjust where necessary. The winner is decided.

Chapter 16:
In the competition room

"One cool Judgement is worth a thousand hasty councils."
Woodrow T Wilson

In this chapter:
- A helping hand
- Out of schedule
- Concentration
- Evaluation
- Completing marking sheets
- Respecting competitors exhibits
- Checking the marks
- Written comments

A judge should never enter the competition room until the steward invites them to do so, and all competitors have left. Once inside the competition room the judge is in total charge.

A helping hand

The steward is there to help the judge, and may assist in measuring any exhibits where necessary, hold bridal designs, or wear headdresses etc. If you do not want the steward present whilst judging then ask them to leave and return once judging has been completed. It is entirely at the discretion of the judge to impose any restrictions they deem fit. It is unwise to enter into discussions with a steward as they are not judges and lack the expertise required to make decisions.

The steward will have numbered each exhibit and the identity of competitors should have been removed. Check that each exhibit has a number first. Check the temperature in the room and the lighting, it may well be that some exhibits benefit from better lighting than others; this should be noted. If the temperature in the room is too high then ask for the heating to be turned down. Curtains may be needed to be drawn to keep out hot sunshine which would affect the quality of the flowers on some exhibits.

It is at the judge's discretion to allow late entries into the competition room. Occasionally competitors have had accidents or hold ups and a willingness to help competitors is essential. However this must be tempered with common sense and if a competition piece arrives long after the judging has started it may not be possible to accommodate the exhibit.

Don't rush into judging immediately; create space and peace around you. Sit down, re read the schedule, quietly concentrating, organise the marking sheets, confidently prepare.

Walk around the designs observing, this preliminary assessment is a calming influence and a visual appraisal bearing the written schedule in mind. Look at how many exhibits are in the room, the quality of them, if they adhere to the schedule. If there is a size requirement now is the time to check.

Out of schedule

Know the rules for 'out of schedule' entries in the competition you are judging. Generally all entries are marked, but in competition heats often the marks for out of schedule exhibits are not carried forward. In other competitions penalty points are given for misdemeanours or faults. Check out what rules apply before the competition.

Before starting to mark, check that the entries are in number sequence around the room. It is very easy to become muddled if the numbers are out of progression. Ask the steward to re arrange the entries if it can be done without disruption to any exhibit.

Concentration

In the competition room a judge needs to bring all of their mental facilities to bear on the exhibits before them, without any deviation whatsoever. No wavering or stray thoughts, purely focusing on the task - giving each design undivided focus. This can be hard if people are talking in the room or there are outside distractions. Silence is preferable in the competition room but not always achievable. Often a judge might be required to assess entries in a public place therefore the ability to switch off from any outside interruptions is essential. This means training the mind, and practising the habit of concentration. The steps to aid concentration are:

- **Planning**. Planning ahead and being organised aids concentration. The knowledge that there is an orderly plan will focus the mind. Planning the judging in a methodical way will aid concentration. Confusion will result if there is no planned timetable, and confusion is when concentration is lost.

- **Relaxation**. Rest and relaxation will aid concentration and give greater mental powers. Stress comes with fatigue and will have a negative effect on a judge's ability to purify thoughts and make decisions. It is a judge's responsibility to make sure they are rested and relaxed, ready for the challenge ahead of them.

- **Mental liberation**. Clearing the mind is essential; it aids a judge to make sound evaluations. Get rid of any external problems or niggling worries or fears. Fear and anxiety have no place in a judge's mind, they will cloud decision making. Serenity is the state the mind should be in.

- **Environment**. Before any competition seek solitude and silence, even if it is only for a few minutes, sit quietly to gather mental energy and strength of concentration. Once the judging starts eliminate outside influences. Extreme focus is achievable wherever judging takes place, if the art of concentration has been practised.

Evaluation

Once you are ready to start the marking process choose a category that will settle you into your judging stride. It may be that Colour is easier to judge first, or perhaps Idea is the preferred opening facet. It is up to you to decide what you are most comfortable with. Confidence is the key to success, faith in your ability to select the winning entry using the correct procedures, and in the manner you are most relaxed with.

Only mark one category at a time, this gives continuity to the marking and it is easier to organise and concentrate on one facet at a time. Flitting from one to another facet is confusing.

Completing marking sheets

When the points have been decided, use a pencil to write down the mark on the marking sheet. It may be that you will need to refer back to a previous mark, or after reflection, alter a mark for consistency in judging. It is easier to rub out a pencil mark.

It is wise to add a few comments or words to the marking sheet. This will remind you of good or bad points when discussing the design with the competitor. Comments should be observations of merits and weaknesses within the exhibit. These comments are always based on the judging facets and not personal preference. Notes can be added as the judging procedure takes place or some judges prefer to make written remarks after judging is completed. It is important to remember that the correct mark is the most important aspect, comments are secondary.

Keep concentrating on the exhibits, to be fair and consistent there should be no distractions, your responsibilities are to the competitors not to onlookers, stewards or fellow judges.

Respecting competitors exhibits

Respect the competitor's exhibits, particularly when examining technique. Each one has some merit, least of all the effort that it has taken to make the exhibit and bring it to the competition. It is upsetting for a competitor to find their efforts have not been rewarded. In fact the poorest entries are often the ones that the judge must pay particular attention to.

When handling exhibits, judges must take extreme care, particularly when checking technique, delicacy of approach is essential. It is not for the judge to destroy or humiliate competitors, rather it is to teach, support and encourage.

Checking marks given

Quietly add the marks up once finished, and then check that your marks agree with the standard of entries in the room. Sometimes the winning entry will surprise you, and then it is worthwhile returning to check the marks in case a mistake has been made. Judges are not infallible and constantly checking marks is essential. Judges should trust their instinct that has been developed with training and experience. Don't be swayed or become indecisive; the judges 'eye' is the most reliable attribute, based on solid factual knowledge. Now is the time to change a mark after further assessment if necessary, this is not a judging error, rather a judge being true to their beliefs and abilities.

A judge is always relieved when there is a clear winner in the competition room. If the two most outstanding entries have the same mark then again this is a time for re-assessment, there can only be one winner. Here deliberation has to be concentrated and acute and this is where judging is at its most complex and demanding. Detailed analysis will test the judge's ability to the full; this is when strength of judging character is essential.

When you are perfectly satisfied with the marks and results ask the steward to verify and check the adding up, and then together write out the competitors mark cards neatly. It is extremely important that another person checks a judge's mark for inaccuracies. Once the marks have been given out if errors are found it reflects on the credibility of the judge.

Written comments

Generally written comments are not added to the competitors mark cards in floristry competitions. However if there is an exception to this, then comments should always be encouraging, with praise for merit and only one or two points of constructive criticism. Tact and diplomacy and legible writing are essential.

Now is the time to sit down quietly, make notes, and reflect on your commentary to the audience and your comments to the competitors. It is advisable to keep away from the competitors until the results have been announced.

There has to be reasonable time given by the organiser to enable the judge to evaluate the entries fairly and expertly. However, this does not mean the judge has unlimited time, there is generally a timescale to work to. It is unprofessional to take too long to judge; for a rule of thumb, generally each piece should be allotted five minutes. Sometimes it is possible to have more time if the entries are low, but if there are twelve entries this means the process will take around one hour, plus time to add up and transpose the marks onto the competitors mark cards. Being decisive, and allocating the marks speedily, is part of a judges training.

Chapter 17:
The commentary

❝ Grasp the subject, the words will follow. ❞
Cato the Elder

In this chapter:
- First impressions
- Conviction and confidence
- Practicing
- Speaking out
- Stage fright
- Structure of the commentary
- The winners' form
- Looking confident
- Using a microphone
- Quick tips for an effective commentary

Of all the things that floristry judges dread most it's the commentary given to an audience of their peers. Most people have a fear of public speaking; yet there are a few simple steps that will make oratory a more enjoyable experience for you and your audience.

First impressions

First impressions do count, how you look will immediately determine how the audience perceives you. The image of a professional, highly trained floristry judge means your attire and grooming should be impeccable. This shows that you respect the audience and they in return will have greater confidence in your commentary. There is power in looking like a true professional, and giving a polished presentation.

Conviction and confidence

The floristry judge is the expert, and the audience of florists are eager to hear the judge's commentary and the judge needs to establish a rapport from the beginning. Developing a good public speaking manner is a skill that takes practice and planning. The key to making an eloquent speech is to be yourself; the audience want you to do well and will know immediately if you are trying to be something you are not. The greatest orators have a natural quality and humility that inspires and touches the emotions.

Practice

Practice speaking at home in front of a mirror. Plan and write down the start of your commentary at home, then practice it. Once the judging is over take a few moments to plan what you will say to the assembled florists' about the winning entries.

There might be an overriding message that you want the audience to remember and take away with them. Focus on the message you want to get across, bringing your own distinctive qualities and personality to the spoken words.

Speaking out

When giving a commentary a floristry judge's voice should be heard by everyone, even those standing at the back of the room. If you have a quiet, weak voice then you must learn to project it. If no one can hear what you say there is absolutely no point in giving a commentary; it only antagonizes and frustrates the audience. If you are prone to saying 'um' or using slang words this will have to be eliminated and it goes without saying that bad language must never be used. Learn to use a variety of words to explain and emphasise points. Never use a complicated word when a short one will do, but do use design vocabulary when talking about floristry entries.

Variation of rhythm and pitch in your voice are essential to convey the message you want to get across. An audience will soon switch off if your voice is monotonous or boring; practice using emotion in your intonation.

Stage fright

George Jessel writes:

'The human brain starts working the moment you are born and never stops until you stand up to speak in public.'

A mental block can suddenly attack when you are stressed, so a few key words written down will trigger the memory.

Armed with all your expert knowledge, plus the winners names and marks, you should have the confidence to give a professional commentary. Nerves can give you unpleasant side effects, a dry mouth, sweating palms, shaking legs and a wobbly voice. Control and self-discipline is the key, keep cool and focused; you are the expert and have the knowledge and enthusiasm to win over the audience.

Structure of the commentary

There should be a start, middle and ending to your commentary. Start with a good opening to attract the audiences' attention, and then keep that attention going with interesting information they want to hear. Humour is a great way to win over an audience, but not at the expense of competitors.

The commentary is not the time to criticise individual competition entries, confine your remarks to general comments and useful tips. Praising the winners is always necessary.

If you are asked to announce the winners leave these till the end of the commentary to build the audience's attention. Always give results in reverse order, third second and then first.

Don't forget to thank the organisers for inviting you and the stewards for their help. Always invite the competitors to talk to you personally in the competition room.

End with a few well-chosen words to sum up. The commentary should never be more than five minutes long, don't waffle on, you might like the sound of your own voice but the audience will switch off if you are not concise and to the point.

The winners' form

Prepare by making a chart that you can add the winners names to, this will save time and avoid confusion. Here is an example, use the title of the competition and instructions to competitors that you will need to read out to the audience and leave spaces for the names of the winners.

Judges competition summary sheet

1. Competition Details: **Date:**

Steward Name: Judge Name:

Competition Location:

2. Competition Task Details:

3. Important information to be read to the competitors:

1. Fresh flowers, foliage and plant material must predominate
2. The judges will be looking for a high standard of composition and technique
3.
4.

4. Competitor Details:

Place	Competitor name shop/address	Comments	Mark
3rd			
2nd			
1st			

Signature:_____(Steward)   _____(Judge)

Look confident

Confidence will show in a calm, still, stance. If you are fidgeting with your hair, your tie, looking at the floor or reading from a script, this all shows you are nervous. Make eye contact with everyone in the room, but don't focus on just one person as this can cause embarrassment. Don't over gesticulate, flapping your arms about will distract from the message you want to get across. Don't use lots of pieces of paper as they may become muddled; only use a clipboard with a single sheet of paper for key points and the winners' names and marks.

If possible ask the steward to hold up the winning entries for the audience to see, you cannot hold your clipboard and floristry exhibits at the same time.

Using a microphone

Using a microphone is essential when talking to a large group of people. Generally a floristry judge will be offered a hand held mike to use. The microphone only amplifies the sound of your voice, if you have a monotonous tone it will not make your voice more interesting, you should still aim for a good vocal range of rhythm and pitch.

Don't make the mistake of refusing a microphone if offered one because you think your voice is loud, the chances are the people at the back of the room will not hear. Make sure the microphone is working properly before use and it is switched on when you go on stage, and switched off when you leave to avoid any private comments being broadcast to the audience.

If the microphone is a clip on type, this should be placed on a lapel or tie approximately 10 centimetres (8 inches) below the chin. If the microphone is too highly placed the sound will be distorted when you move your head.

When using a hand held mike, always stand up straight, good posture is essential to improve the quality of your voice. Generally hold the microphone 5 to 6 cm (two or three inches) from your mouth although this might vary depending on the make of the microphone. Never crowd the microphone as this will distort your voice and could give irritating feedback. Keep in mind that if you turn your head away from the microphone it will not pick up your voice.

Remember that the microphone picks up every sound and will amplify every breath and mispronunciation you make. So controlled breathing and clear diction is essential.

The microphone is a tool to aid you but the delivery and content of your commentary is up to you; the focus is always on the quality of what you have to say and the way you present it.

Quick tips for giving an effective commentary

- First impressions count, look well groomed and professional.
- Smile, be friendly, natural and relaxed.
- Remember the audience are generally professional florists never talk down to them.
- Develop an introduction that will catch the attention of the audience.
- Give confidence; show your conviction and enthusiasm.
- Don't waffle; keep the commentary sharp, short and interesting.
- Find the right words; use a range of vocabulary and design terminology.
- Avoid repetition by using differing words and explanations for the same terminology.
- Make eye contact with everyone.
- NEVER criticize entries in the commentary; give general points for improving all the entries and highlight interesting points.
- Always read the schedule to the audience, with a short explanation.
- A commentary should have a beginning, middle and end.
- Speak out clearly, and use a microphone when available.
- NEVER discuss personal likes or dislikes. Let it be clear that the judging has been made according to the recognised rules.
- Always be polite and thank the steward and organisers.
- Give out winners in reverse order 3rd then 2nd finally 1st.
- Always invite competitors into the judging room for individual discussions.
- Finish with some memorable and inspirational words.

Chapter 18:
Talking to competitors

" If your actions inspire others to dream more, learn more, do more and become more, you are a leader. "
John Quincy Adams

In this chapter:
- Points on how to give constructive criticism
- Vocabulary
- Using descriptive words
- Words to inspire

At the end of the commentary, the judge must always invite competitors into the competition room to have a personal appraisal of their competition entry. This is where the work of a floristry judge is at its most important. Here you can inspire and motivate, praise and give constructive advice. The judge's aim is to create a feel good, memorable experience for every competitor, no matter whether they came first or last in the competition. There is always something to praise, and the fact that the competitor has taken the trouble to enter the competition needs recognition.

A smiling welcoming face will help to calm the competitor's nerves. Listen carefully to what the competitor has to say about their work, make eye contact, show you care about every single person, give praise first and then take the time to explain one or two mistakes and give constructive criticism and advice.

Key points on how to give competitors constructive criticism.

- Always have a smiling welcome.
- Start the discussion with a compliment.
- Empathise with the competitor, show you understand where the competitor is coming from and the problems encountered.
- Be a good listener.
- Use eye contact to show you are paying attention.
- Be kind and considerate.
- Use descriptive words to stimulate and encourage.
- Never belittle a competitor.
- Show competitors the judging facets; often they have never seen them.
- Explain where and why points have been deducted.
- Don't overload the competitor with too many criticisms; focus on one or to main points only.

- Never use personal phrases such as 'I like.' The marks you have given have nothing to do with personal preference, they are based on the analysis of the facets - stick to these.
- Soften the words used when giving any negative analysis and try to offer a design or technical solution.
- Don't harp on, make the point and move on.
- Always use design vocabulary.
- Try to embolden and inspire the competitors to enter the next competition.
- Remember that some of the competitors will have travelled a long distance and may want too get away quickly, don't spent to long with the first competitor as the last will have left the room frustrated before you get to their entry.

Vocabulary

The words a judge uses when speaking both in the commentary and in individual discussions with the competitors will have a profound effect on the way the judging is received and the way you are perceived. Finding the right words will build a rapport and can motivate and inspire. Remember that florists' are visual artists and imagery is important.

Use descriptive words

> If words are not correct then what is said is not what is meant, And what ought to be done remains undone.
> *Confucius*

Using descriptive words that paint vivid pictures in the competitors mind will help them retain the information you give them. Using design vocabulary is important, but often the competitor will not understand the design phraseology and will need an explanation of the words. This doesn't mean you have to use long convoluted words; rather simple, clear sharp phrases that conjure up imagery. Repeating the same words over and over again becomes boring, and competitors become unconvinced if similar words are used when talking to each competitor. Try to avoid hackneyed sayings and think of new ways to illustrate a meaning by using fresh clear articulation. Try to use metaphors to conjure up pictures in the head.

For example, yellow is not just yellow it is ochre, sunshine, ripened wheat, golden, zesty lemon, primrose, saffron. Pink is Barbie, raspberry, mulberry, magenta, fuchsia, plum, rose; all these names are more than just yellow or pink, and they trigger a vision in the head.

Lets look at a design element, take repetition for example, and think of a metaphor to help competitors understand why repetition is a great design tool. The competitor might understand better if you asked them to think of a stately home with a row of tall columns at equal distances outside the entrance, or a viaduct with equidistant arches, or a row of identical dresses of the same colour and style in a shop.

It might be better to say that repetition is a recurring echo like the bass beat in a piece of music that moves you on through the melody. Relate this to floristry, where repetition is a powerful tool, a device to help the eye navigate through a floral design.

In technique, finish is a very important facet, but many competitors may think that this means stopping on time. How to convey the meaning of finish then? It's the extra special top layer of quality. If buttons are missing from a jacket, the hems of trousers are ragged, nail varnish is chipped then there is a scruffy appearance and this is a lack of finish. This also applied to floristry with untidy wiring or taping, scruffy foliage etc. If everything is perfectly polished and executed neatly then this is perfect finish.

Think of ways to explain the design terminology in one illuminating sentence that will be understood by competitors.

Words to inspire

Learn to use descriptive words that will inspire, educate, motivate and explain. There are many Internet sites that have examples of descriptive words to use when critiquing art and design. Make a list of useful words that you can carry with you on judging assignments; these will be a trigger to use when searching for the right word to describe the physical characteristics of design.

Words to describe line

Vertical	Horizontal	Diagonal
Zigzag	Curving	Short
Straight	Wide	Meandering
Interrupted	Blurred	Broken
Controlled	Parallel	Concave
Sharp	Rolling	Contoured
Geometric	Concentric	

Descriptive words for textures

Flat	Furry	Dotted
Ridged	Shiny	Glossy
Rough	Prickly	Smooth
Silky	Tufted	Velvety
Soft	Bumpy	Knobbly
Woolly	Downy	Fluffy

List of descriptive words

A
Absolutely	Absorbing	Abundance	Ace	Active
Admirable	Arc	Agree	Accomplished	Average
Alive	Amazing	Appealing	Appropriate	Attraction
Artistic	Attractive			

B
Blameless	Beautiful	Best	Better	Bad
Brief	Bright	Brilliant	Breezy	Brimming

C
Confusing	Contrived	Conflicting	Charming	Chic
Clever	Clean	Clear	Colourful	Commendable
Complementary	Confidence	Connoisseur	Cool	Competent
Coy	Conforming	Crisp	Consistent	

D
Dazzling	Debonair	Delicate	Delightful	Delightful
Deluxe	Distinguished	Disjointed	Diamond	Divine
Discerning	Distinctive	Dynamic		

E
Elegant	Exciting	Effervescent	Efficient	Energetic
Enhance	Enchanting	Enormous	Essential	Enticing
Elaborate	Eye-catching	Excellent	Exceptional	Exciting
Exclusive	Exhilaration	Exotic	Expert	Exquisite
Extol				

F
Fair	Fine	Fantastic	Fashionable	Fascinating
Flawless	Focused	Fetching	Finest	Finesse
Fragrant	Fizz	Flair	Flattering	Fresh
Flourishing	Free	Fun		

G
Good	Great	Genius	Gentle	glamourous
Glorious	Glowing	Goodness	Gorgeous	Graceful
Grand	Great			

H
Heartwarming

I
Imaginative	Ideal	Immaculate	Impressive	Incredible
Inspirational	Instant	Interesting	Invigorating	Impressive
Inviting	Irresistible	Incomparable	Innovative	Inventive
Inappropriate	Incompatible	Inconsistent	Improved	

K
Know-how Keenest

L
Legendary	Light	Lingering	Lacking	Lovely
Luscious	Luxurious			

M
Magic	Matchless	Modern	Maximum	Memorable
Mighty	More			

N
Natural	Nice	Nutritious

O
Outstanding	Opulent	Original	Outrageous

P
Pristine	Proficient	Palatial	Paradise	Perfect
Passionate	Peak	Pearl	Pleasant	Prestigious
Plump	Plus	Popular	Positive	Powerful
Precious	Prime	Pure	Pride	Proud

Q
Quintessential	Quality	Quenching

R
Radiant	Ravishing	Refined	Refreshing	Remarkable
Reliable	Renowned	Rhymetic	Restful	Rewarding
Rich	Right			

S
Safe	Skillful	Satisfactory	Skilled	Seductive
Superior	Sensitive	Sensational	Serene	Supreme
Superb	Superlative	Share	Sufficient	Suitable
Static	Silver	Simple	Subtle	Sizzling
Skillful	Slick	Successful	Stunning	Salute
Smooth	Strong	Spotless	Sparkling	Special
Spectacular	Streamlined	Spicy	Splendid	Spherical
Solid	Spruce	Stylish	Sun	Supreme
Symphony				

T
Terrific	Talented	Thrilling	Timeless	Tasteful
Transformation	Tender	Traditional	Tempting	Thriving
Top	Treat	Trust		

U
Ultimate	Unconventional	Unnatural	Unrelated	Unrivalled
Unblemished	Unique			

V
Valuable	Vigorous	Visualize	Vital	Vivacious
Valued	Versatile	V.I.P.		

W
Wonderful	Well-prepared	Well suited	Warm	Welcoming
Wealth				

Use this page to add your own descriptive words to explain the Principles and Elements of Design.

Additional words to explain:

Composition:

Technique:

Colour:

Idea:

Chapter 19:
Team and open judging

" None of us are as smart as all of us. "
Ken Blanchard

In this chapter:
- Lead judge
- How to be a dream team judge
- Open judging

There are often times when floristry judges are required to work together as a panel at competitions. In a final competition, where heats have previously taken place, there are often three or more judges. Generally, judges are required to evaluate separately on three of the facets, Idea, Colour and Composition, but on the fourth facet - Technique, judges come together to mark collectively.

There is merit in judging Technique as a team. When there are six judges, if each one handles the competition piece several times, it can result in unnecessary damage to the design; also technique and workmanship are tangible elements, therefore they are more objective to judge. Working on the premise that more heads are better than one, there will be added accuracy, and each judge will bring a fresh approach to the task. This doesn't mean to say that there cannot be a lively debate about any aspect that there is disagreement on. However, professionalism and respect for judging colleagues is essential and listening carefully to the other judges' points of view is paramount. It's essential when working as a group that every judge contributes to the decision; each judge's opinion is important. Open communication is the foundation to successful team judging.

Lead judge

Generally when judging in a team there will be a lead judge who will steer the panel, avoiding unnecessary and time consuming debates, and who assists in coming to a joint decision. The lead judge is generally a very experienced, respected judge, who has knowledge of team judging, great communication and listening skills, and the ability to arrive by consensus at a marking decision, which all judges are happy with. In some instances the lead judge will have the casting vote.

There will be a few minutes to look around the competition exhibit and visually appraise it, and then the lead judge will generally, (depending on how much time there is) ask each judge in turn to give a critical assessment before taking a vote on a mark. If there is no lead judge, then each judge takes it in turn to fulfill this role as they make there way around the competition entries.

In some cases the whole competition is judged using the team method, this is helpful when time is limited and there are a large number of entries to judge in the competition.

How to be a dream team judge

- Communication is the key, don't keep quiet then regret it later.
- Likewise don't hog all the conversation, know when to keep quiet and allow everyone to speak.
- Listen carefully to what the other judges say, only comment when necessary.
- Give clear reasons for any decision you make.
- Be honest and truthful, team judging is not about gaining points, but coming to the correct decision.
- Be professional and friendly at all times.
- Respect the opinions of your fellow team judges.
- Enjoy and learn from the team judging experience.
- Never criticize the marks given, or the judging, after the competition.

Open judging

In some major world floristry competitions open judging has been adopted, and a number of countries are now using this approach in their national floristry competitions. Open judging is when floristry judges walk freely amongst the competitors whilst they are making their entries; the judges then evaluate and mark the work as it is being made. The arguments for this type of judging are compelling, although not without controversy.

One of the reasons for open judging is to make the competitions more appealing to spectators. Showing the general public how floristry is made and assessed makes a competition more interesting to watch. Often the competition closes and the room is evacuated for judging to take place, and then the complex work of the judge is hidden from view. The audience is left wondering who has won and lose interest. Floristry competitions have a purpose to promote and encourage excellence in floristry, but also a wider responsibility to advance and support florists through publicity. Making floristry competitions more accessible and interesting for customers has to go hand in hand with the quality of floristry competitions and judging.

Another important consideration is that the results of the competition can be given much quicker, therefore eliminating a lengthy wait to announce the winners. Also on the technical side open judging gives the judge the opportunity to see the construction of a design, therefore giving valuable insight into how the competition entry has been made. On the negative side some competitors do not trust judges to be objective, even a few judges do not have the confidence in their own impartiality. However, in test judging exercises done in Europe using both methods, the winner has almost always been the same using both methods. It's finding a balance between objective judging, happy competitors, and placing more emphasis on the enjoyment of the audience.

Chapter 20:
The competition schedule

"Think like a wise man but communicate in the language of the people."
William Butler Yeats

In this chapter:
- What is a floristry competition schedule?
- Schedule preparation
- Inspiring schedules
- Discussion
- Surprise/Mystery competitions
- Key points when writing competition schedules

What is a floristry competition schedule?

A floristry competition schedule is an instruction to the competitor to make a required floral design. It's the only way to tell the competitor what the judge will be expecting to see in the competition room. Every floristry competition has a purpose, a task to be fulfilled by the competitor.

Telling competitors what to do in a written schedule must be done in clear and simple prose. Writing a schedule is a job that requires precision, making it easy for the competitors to process the information without complicating the route with unnecessary wording.

Schedule preparation

All judges must undertake the task of writing floristry competition schedules. It's unfair to leave this work to a few stalwarts, plus differing judges can put a new slant on an old theme, or have original ideas that can inspire the competitor.

When it comes to the written word, florists are generally visual processors, they think in pictures and colours, therefore the competition schedule must inspire and conjure images in the head. It is important to write precise instructions with no needless wording. Writing tight sentences that cannot be construed incorrectly, eliminating ambiguous or misleading words is essential.

If any competitor is disqualified it is generally because the competition schedule has been worded badly, and the competitor does not understand the instructions. Therefore schedule writing must never be undertaken lightly, it is the most important part of the competition and an essential part of a judge's work.

Writing competition schedules is a minefield, and great thought must be applied to every schedule to avoid competitors becoming disheartened.

The degree of difficulty in the schedule will depend on whom the competition is targeted at. If it is a beginner's class then obviously the task will have to be within the capabilities of these competitors. Too difficult, and it will deter the competitors from entering the competition.

Know your subject and keep the competitor in mind. Before you start, define the competitor and identify what you want from them. Think of the schedule as a map that the competitor must navigate. Use short familiar words and active verbs.

Inspiring schedules

There has to be some stimulus within the schedule, an inspirational incentive for competitors to enter the competition, and the more experienced the competitor the more necessary this is. Competitors should feel excited and motivated when they first see the competition schedule and experience an urge to create.

Competitor schedules should never be restrictive, they should allow for the competitors creativity and should be as open as possible.
Start a schedule with:

'Create a bridal bouquet,'
and the judge must know that only designs with a handle will be acceptable. If this is what is required fine, but often it is better to write:

'Create a bridal design to be carried by the bride on her wedding day,'
then this does not restrict the competitor to making a bouquet only and they know that this is to be carried on the actual wedding day.

Similarly a schedule that asks competitors to:

'Produce a body accessory for a bride to wear,'
the competitors and judges must know what is acceptable. Does this mean all types of body adornments, from headdresses to ankle decoration? This could also be a bride wearing something for a hen party, or an occasion leading up to the wedding; it doesn't necessarily have to be on her wedding day. Be more specific about the commands that are given to the competitor.

If you want the competitors to make only necklaces then you must state this.

'Make a necklace for a bride to wear on her wedding day.'

Careful choice of words is essential, for example, the use of words such as, contemporary or modern, are ambiguous and ask for problems. Who can say what is contemporary? What is current to one person is old fashioned to another. Let the competitor decide what design to create.

Stipulating a colour scheme can also be disastrous. 'Make an all white arrangement,' for example, what about green foliage? There are not many pure white flowers either. Think of all the implications not only for the competitors but for the judges also.

Generally at the end of the schedule two sentences will appear to instruct the competitor.

'The judges will expect fresh flower and plant material to predominate.'
'The judges will be looking for a high standard of design and technical skill.'

These are clear instructions to the competitor to tell them what is expected.

Always send out a copy of the marking facets with the competition schedule. The competitors need to know how the marks will be allocated.

Often, when there is more than one design to make, the overall competition will have a theme and this may run through all the designs to be made. Again the theme should be a spur to ignite the competitors' creativity.

Discussion

Often there are competition heats taking place around the country, all using the same schedule, but with different judges attending them. To avoid any misunderstanding, discussion between all the judges is imperative as everyone interprets the schedule differently. It's very important that the judges talk to one another and have a clear brief, and so knowing exactly what is allowed. This will avoid disqualifications and unpleasant scenes after the competition. Whoever writes the competition schedule should also add a judge's brief to be circulated to all judges. If any judge is unsure, then asking fellow judges is essential.

Surprise or mystery competitions

Surprise or mystery competitions are different to other competitions because the competitor does not generally have a written schedule. It's a secret until all the competitors open their boxes of flowers and sundries at the same time. A judge or experienced competitor is generally asked to put together the surprise package. Assembling the mystery flowers, foliage and sundries takes real skill to ensure that there are creative materials for the competitors to work with.

Chapter 20: The competition schedule

Key points for writing schedules

- Every floristry competition has an air or a purpose.
- The schedule wording must be concise and simple.
- There should be careful phrasing to eliminate any misunderstanding by the competitor or judge.
- Strip down words to analyse their meanings, this will help to eliminate any ambiguous or confusing sentences.
- Competition schedules should not be restrictive, they should always allow for creativity.
- Schedules should inspire competitors to enter competitions. Use words that will ignite the imagination of the competitor.
- Think of the level of the competitor; junior competitions may require easier schedules.
- Explore the possibilities of the schedule from a competitors and judges point of view.
- Try to avoid any factual limitations i.e. 'to be delivered.' A grand piano can be delivered, so to be delivered is irrelevant.
- Try not to introduce any monetary value into schedules, as the cost of materials varies enormously around the country, making it impossible to judge constructively.
- Think of the practical elements of displaying competition pieces at confined venues.
- After writing a schedule show it to another judge, in confidence, for their comments.
- Mystery or surprise competitions need specialist preparation.
- Always send the marking facets out with any competition schedule.
- Always be fair to the competitor.

Chapter 21:
Overseas judging

I like to see a man proud of the place in which he lives. I like to see a man live so that his place will be proud of him.
Abraham Lincoln

In this chapter:
* Judging facets
* Material respect
* Communication

It's a great honour for a judge to be asked to represent their country in an overseas competition. If afforded this privilege, it's also a great responsibility, for the judge is an ambassador not only for their fellow judges, but they are their countries envoy. Acting with dignity, fairness and independence, and taking care not to undermine the judging role needs maturity of character. Therefore floristry judges with many years experience are generally afforded this privilege. It's important that judges go to as many overseas competitions as possible, before taking a judging assignment abroad.

Judging facets may vary

In Europe, the judge may find that the judging facets are very similar to Great Britain's, although European countries often have a factor called 'Material Respect,' in many free expression, hand tied and arrangement schedules. However, Material Respect is not marked in bridal and accessory schedules where wiring and control is required.

Material respect

Respecting the flowers and foliage used is essential in all floral design. Over manipulation, mutilation of natural materials and extreme contortion of flowers can have a detrimental effect on the design.

Study the marking schedule before the competition to ensure you are familiar with the entire wording. It may be that the marks for each facet are different from the way you are used to working so careful analysis is essential.

Always request a competition schedule and a list of any questions and their answers that the competitors have asked, together with the marking facets. Do your homework well in advance, and take with you all the necessary stationary you may require.

Communication

It may be that you have to communicate through an interpreter. Hopefully the interpreter will have some floristry knowledge together with bilingual skills, so that your message is fully understood and not misconstrued. Careful, simple, explanations are imperative. When a foreign language is used and judges are talking between themselves always ask what is being discussed, it is easy to be out of the loop and miss vital judging information.

The basic principles of good design are practiced throughout the world, so whilst the implementation of the competition may vary from country to country, the floristry judges will all be looking for the same building blocks that makes a floristry design a creative work of art.